The Wedding Planner

The Wedding Planner

ANTONIA SWINSON

with photography by
Caroline Arber and Polly Wreford

RYLAND
PETERS
& SMALL
LONDON NEW YORK

First published in Great Britain in 2001.
This new edition published in 2006
by Ryland Peters & Small
20–21 Jockey's Fields
London WC1R 4BW

ISBN-10: 1-84597-194-9
ISBN-13: 978-1-84597-194-6

A CIP record for this book is available
from the British Library.

Printed in China

Designer Vicky Holmes

Senior Editor Clare Double

Commissioning Editor Annabel Morgan

Location Research Manager Kate Brunt

Location Researcher Sarah Hepworth

Production Meryl Silbert, Deborah Wehner

Art Director Gabriella Le Grazie

Publishing Director Alison Starling

INTRODUCTION A wedding that runs smoothly from beginning to end doesn't do so without a great deal of work. It's a highly complex social event and one which involves a daunting array of different elements. You'll probably feel like an accomplished juggler by the end of it all. There is also the pressure of expectation: every bride wants her day to be perfect and for her guests to think it's the best wedding they've ever been to.

The only answer is to be organized and to become good at delegating. Traditionally, the bride's parents planned and paid for everything, but nowadays the burden, both organizational and financial, is normally spread more evenly and grooms are often just as involved in decisions as their brides. Nonetheless, someone has to oversee all the arrangements, ticking off all the tasks as they're done, and this is still normally the bride. That's where this book comes in. Treat it as your friendly guide, leading you through the maze of wedding planning and etiquette. There are checklists you can tick off, places to make notes and lots of ideas, plus a comprehensive address book of wedding companies and services.

Remember, though, that getting married is about two people. It's an opportunity for a wonderful celebration, but it would still be a wedding just with you two and a minister or registrar. Don't be so wildly ambitious that the day begins to take on a life of its own and threatens to take over yours. Organizing your wedding should be enjoyable, not a terrible burden. Truly happy weddings are rarely the ones which have had the most money thrown at them. The spirit of the day and the people who share it are more important than pounds and pence.

Have a wonderful wedding!

Top **Rings have been exchanged as love tokens for thousands of years and are a worldwide symbol of married status.**

Above **Wedding cakes were once fertility symbols and many couples still keep the top tier for the christening of their first child.**

Above right **The Victorians popularized the language of flowers. Wedding posies were originally carried to ward off evil spirits.**

Below right **Rice has given way to more decorative forms of confetti, from tiny paper shapes to rose petals and bubbles.**

Whatever the current vogue, most weddings incorporate elements of tradition.

Top and above left **The wedding dress is the focus of much attention on the day. With a huge choice of designs on the market, and a range of prices to match, finding 'the one' should be within the reach of every bride.**

Above right **Few things say 'wedding' more than a marquee and a glorious summer's day.**

Right **Many couples still take their vows in church, but there are now thousands of venues in England and Wales licensed to hold civil weddings.**

WEDDING TRADITIONS

♥ Bouquets were originally posies of herbs, carried to ward off evil spirits.

♥ The verse 'Something old, something new…' refers to the bride's passage from her old life to her new one. 'Something borrowed' means that marriage involves sharing; 'something blue' alludes to the colour's association with constancy; 'and a silver sixpence in your shoe' refers to the hope of prosperity in marriage.

♥ White weddings were an invention of the Victorians, before whom brides simply wore their best dress, sometimes with a white ribbon attached to symbolize purity.

♥ Veils were thought to keep away evil spirits, who would be confused by not being able to see the bride.

♥ Chimney sweeps are associated with the hearth and home, and it's therefore thought to be good luck to kiss one on the way to the ceremony.

♥ The wedding ring symbolizes everlasting love. It's thought that the ancient Egyptians started the practice of wearing one on the third finger of the left hand – they believed that the vein in that finger ran straight to the heart.

♥ Throwing confetti has its roots in the Roman period, when guests threw nuts at newlyweds to symbolize a fruitful marriage.

♥ Cutting a cake at a wedding was once thought to ensure a fruitful marriage. Keeping a piece of cake is supposed to guarantee that your husband stays faithful.

♥ The honeymoon gets its name from the tradition of newlyweds drinking honeyed mead (a symbol of life and fertility) until the moon waned.

♥ Wedding receptions have their roots in the medieval period, when the groom had to demonstrate that he could support his wife by giving gifts of food and drink to his in-laws.

Planning your wedding

Being organized is the key to enjoying your engagement and big day.
Decide what style of wedding you'd like, don't panic, and get started!

Wedding style

Weddings are rooted in tradition, so they share common elements – the dress, the flowers, the cake and so on. These provide countless ways to be creative and make your wedding reflect your taste.

Inspiration

Think of your wedding as a whole and make sure that all the elements complement each other: the dress, the groom's outfit, the attendants' clothes, the flowers, the cake, the table decorations, the stationery. The starting point is normally the bride's dress, from which springs the choice of attendants' outfits and flowers. But there are other sources of inspiration. The time of year often suggests certain colours and themes: blues and yellows in spring; fiery reds, oranges and yellows in autumn; tables decorated with coloured eggs at an Easter wedding; holly and ivy wreaths at a Christmas celebration. If you're marrying in summer, you could adopt the rose as your theme. Your reception venue might set the mood, a castle suggesting a medieval or fairy-tale theme. Shared interests or passions could be another starting point. Perhaps you've been to India together and want the reception to be a blaze of saffron yellows and hot pinks. You may simply want to have a classic white wedding, from your dress down to the confetti. Keeping it simple is often the most stylish choice.

Colour

Colour is an easy way to give your wedding a sense of continuity. Most brides still wear white, though usually not pure white but a shade from ivory to cream. White is an excellent foil for other colours. Choose one accent shade for a

Pastel shades and pretty tableware create a look that's traditional and romantic without being old-fashioned.

Above left **Flowers set the scene with gentle colour and scent. Cottage-garden favourites used** *en masse* **have great charm.**

Above centre **Pretty effects are often easy to create: here, the napkins have been tied with lengths of ribbon and adorned with a single bloom.**

Above right and below **Most caterers and hire companies offer various styles of table linen, glassware, china and cutlery, allowing you a bit of creative licence.**

simple but stylish scheme and use it for details such as ribbon round the bouquets, the icing on the cake, flowers, embroidery on your dress, candles and the groom's waistcoat. Gold or silver adds richness and sparkle. You could choose a single pastel: baby blue, ice-cream pink, lemon yellow, mint green or lilac. A touch of a dark shade such as rich pink adds drama, or you could go for the ultimate contrast of black and white. A single colour also looks good used in a variety of shades. Pink is the obvious choice, since many traditional wedding flowers – roses, carnations, lilies, peonies – come in glorious shades of it, from pale to deep. Colour can prompt a wedding theme: tropical travellers could have hot-coloured flowers and tables draped in bright sari fabric with an Indian feast. You might want a more complex colour scheme and to use shades that contrast with or complement each other. For instance, contrasting partners include yellow and blue, and pink and green. Complementary ones are pink and blue, and yellow and orange. If you're using contrasting colours, keep one paler than the other in order to keep the effect soft.

Stylish colour schemes ♥ Lemon yellow and hyacinth blue, or sunflower yellow with baby blue. ♥ Deep pink and mint green, or powder pink with forest green. ♥ Sugared-almond pastels – pale pink, blue, green, yellow, lilac. ♥ Pale mauve and soft, lime greens. ♥ Soft yellow, orange, apricot and russet (an autumnal scheme). ♥ Ruby red, gold and forest green (rich, wintry colours). ♥ Rich pinks and rose reds (but use deep shades with care). ♥ Silver and pale blue or lilac. ♥ Rose pink and gold.

Themed weddings These are not to everyone's taste, but you may love the thought of being a medieval lord and lady for the day. A venue may suggest a historical theme, or you may have a passion for a particular period. Couples have been known to persuade their guests to hire medieval costume, entertaining them with troubadours and a hog-roast banquet. However, this takes some doing and it's easier to introduce historical touches selectively. This might mean fleur-de-lis embroidery on your dress and his waistcoat, and a cake castle. Weddings by the sea suggest a holiday feel. You could give the day a blue and white colour scheme, tuck a shell into each guest's napkin as a keepsake, serve fish at your meal and float candles in bowls of water as table centrepieces. The seasons often inspire themes. If you marry in December, Christmas can come early with mulled wine, wreaths of holly and red roses, and tables decked with baubles and crackers. Or perhaps you'll have a midsummer night's dream, with little bridesmaids dressed as fairies, a marquee festooned with fairy lights, lots of romantic summer flowers and a firework display. A wedding is a unique opportunity to throw a wonderful party. If you're ever going to indulge your fantasies, now's the time to do it.

This cool, modern reception incorporates a hint of Eastern aesthetics.

Opposite top **The glassware is simple and elegant, with clean-cut lines.**

Opposite below **A fresh, modern look is created by the combination of natural materials – wood, flowers and foliage – with touches of harder-edged ones such as chrome. The place** settings are chic and sophisticated, but special touches such as candles in frosted-glass holders soften the look, setting the scene for a celebration.

Above **A vase of arum lilies echoes the simplicity of Eastern flower arranging.**

Below **More hints of exoticism with napkin rings made of glossy, tropical leaves tied with grass.**

Countdown to the day It hardly needs saying that the earlier you make arrangements, the better chance you have of being able to book the best reception venues, photographers, florists and so on. However, engagements seem to be getting shorter, so many brides don't have much time to organize everything. Resist the urge to panic and get cracking as soon as possible. You may have to be flexible, though, and have other dates and ideas ready in case venues and services are already booked. If some arrangements don't go as planned, don't let them overshadow what will still be a wonderful day.

Once you're engaged

☐ Set a date for the wedding. You may want to put an announcement in a local or national newspaper.

☐ Fix your budget and decide what your priorities are. Discuss who will organize and pay for what and make sure everyone is clear about what has been decided.

☐ Book the venue for the ceremony – church, civil venue or register office – and have a meeting with the person who will marry you.

☐ Book your reception venue or marquee and caterer (remember to put everything in writing) and discuss food and drink.

☐ Book musicians for ceremony or reception.

☐ Draw up a guest list in consultation with both sets of parents.

☐ Order wedding stationery.

☐ Book a photographer and videographer (if you're marrying in church, check whether you're allowed to photograph or film inside).

☐ Arrange your wedding transport. You may need cars to the church or venue, from there to the reception venue and for going away.

☐ Order your cake.

☐ Choose your bridesmaids, pageboys, best man and ushers.

☐ Start looking at wedding dresses and accessories, and outfits for your attendants. Remember that it can take several months for a dress to be made to measure.

☐ Order your flowers.

☐ Start to plan your honeymoon. If you're going in high season, book as early as possible.

☐ Investigate local accommodation for guests who are travelling long distances. Reserve rooms in good time and inform guests of this when you send out your invitations.

Three months before the day

☐ Organize a wedding gift list.

☐ Buy your wedding rings.

☐ Run through the form of the wedding service. Choose your music and readings (for a church ceremony, discuss with your minister; for a civil wedding, check with the registrar).

☐ If you're going to send wedding cake to people who can't attend, order boxes.

☐ Arrange to hire formalwear for the male members of the wedding party.

- [ ] Choose your going-away clothes if you're having them. (On the day, someone will need to make sure that your dress and your groom's suit are taken home once you've left.)
- [ ] Make sure your honeymoon plans are finalized and that you've organized visas, inoculations, travel insurance and currency.
- [ ] Send invitations out at least six weeks before the day (eight or even 12 is safer) and, as replies come in, make a list of who is coming. Remember that an invitation should be sent to the groom's parents. It's also courteous to invite the officiating minister.
- [ ] Buy gifts for your helpers on the day, such as bridesmaids, pageboys, best man, ushers and both your mothers.
- [ ] Think about taking out wedding insurance.
- [ ] If you are changing your name on your passport, send it off in plenty of time. Others to inform include your employer, bank, building society, insurance company, the Inland Revenue, the Department of Social Security and your GP.
- [ ] Practise your make-up. See your hairdresser to try styles. Book your appointment for the day.
- [ ] Book your first-night hotel.

One month before

- [ ] Give your ushers instructions for the day. It might be useful to give them brief written notes.
- [ ] As presents arrive, write thank-you letters.

- [ ] Confirm all arrangements for the reception, catering, entertainment, transport and so on and check the final number of guests.
- [ ] Draw up a seating plan.
- [ ] Have your final fittings for your dress if necessary and try on your whole outfit, with underwear and accessories, before the day.
- [ ] Arrange a wedding rehearsal.
- [ ] Check that the best man knows what his duties for the day are.
- [ ] Arrange the hen night and stag night.

One week before

- [ ] Remind your fiancé to write his speech and write one yourself if you're going to speak.
- [ ] Make final confirmations with your reception venue and caterer, photographer, florist, cake maker and so on, and with your travel agent or tour operator. Make sure that anyone who needs it has a contact number for you, and that they know exactly where to deliver goods.
- [ ] Pack for your honeymoon. Ask the best man to make sure that your luggage is put in your going-away car or is sent ahead to your hotel.
- [ ] Wear your wedding shoes around the house to ensure they'll be comfortable on the day.
- [ ] Have a final try-on of your wedding clothes.
- [ ] Remind the best man to return hired formalwear straight after the wedding.
- [ ] Have the wedding rehearsal and double check that all your helpers know what they're meant to be doing on the day.

On the day Don't leave yourself with any jobs to do. Instead, give someone else the responsibility of receiving the bouquets and buttonholes, seeing that the orders of service are ready to be given out, that the cake has been delivered and so on. It's important that you should be able to concentrate on getting ready. Make sure you have some time completely on your own before the wedding to gather your thoughts and take some deep, relaxing breaths. Take a conscious decision to enjoy every minute of your wedding – it goes all too quickly.

When you're back Get on with your thank-you letters if you didn't do them before the day. Make sure all hired formalwear was returned and see to any outstanding bills. Clean and store your dress. If you want to change your name on bank accounts and so on but haven't yet done so, do it now.

General planning tips

♥ If the demands of your job leave you with no time to organize your wedding, you could hire a professional wedding coordinator. Establishing how good their experience and contacts are is crucial, so ask if they can provide references. Most offer a free, no-obligation preliminary meeting. Make sure you understand exactly how their charges work before you commit yourself.

♥ Don't be afraid to delegate.

♥ Although you'll want to take into account the feelings and views of your family, it's your day and ultimately you must do what you want. You can't please everyone all the time.

♥ Try to have a day or two off before the wedding to give yourself a chance to wind down from work.

♥ Get everything in writing, including quotes and estimates, and confirmation of arrangements with suppliers. Keep all your paperwork in a file so you can find things easily.

The budget Deciding how much you can afford to spend on your wedding is the key to the whole event, so make it the first thing you do.

Traditionally, the bride's parents organized and paid for everything. Nowadays it's much more common for both sets of parents to contribute or for couples to pay for everything themselves. Work out who will pay for what and make sure that everyone is clear about what has been decided. Bear in mind that if someone is paying for something, they may feel that it gives them a say in how the money is spent. Be realistic about money: a wedding that's going to leave you financially compromised isn't a good start to married life.

Most couples allocate their biggest chunk of money – perhaps around 50 per cent – to their reception. There is an obligation to look after guests well, so don't overreach yourself. The other main areas, namely wedding clothes and accessories, music, photography, flowers, and other miscellaneous items (invitations, favours and so on), will probably account for about 10 per cent each.

Once you've set a budget, put it on paper and stick to it. Don't forget to add a safety net for unforeseen costs. Get at least a couple of quotes for

every service and remember that, to get an accurate figure, provide as much information as possible, such as the number of guests. Read all quotes carefully, including the small print. Watch out for hidden extras such as delivery costs or charges for extra staff. Use your common sense: if a quote looks unusually low, ask yourself why. Make sure that all subsequent dealings with your suppliers are in writing and check when they need to know final numbers. Set up a file for all your quotes and bills as they come in. Keep a running total so you know how on or off target you are.

You'll almost certainly have to pay a deposit when you accept a quote. The amount varies, but could be up to 50 per cent of the bill. The balance will be due around the time of the wedding. Check whether you need to arrange for payments while you are away on honeymoon.

Cutting costs Focus your resources on the things that matter the most to you. You could ask people to contribute in some way towards the wedding rather than buy you a present. You may have a cookery-mad friend who's happy to make your cake; a dexterous mother who wants to make your bridesmaids' dresses; a friend with a well-stocked garden who's happy to do your flower arrangements; or someone with a camcorder who'll video the day for you. There are cost-cutting tips in each chapter of this book.

Who pays for what Below is the traditional breakdown of who pays for what, but how you arrange things is up to you.

The bride's parents

- ♥ press announcements
- ♥ the bride's outfit
- ♥ flowers for the ceremony and reception
- ♥ photographer and videographer
- ♥ transport
- ♥ the reception
- ♥ wedding stationery
- ♥ the cake

The groom

- ♥ all ceremony or church fees (including organist and choir)
- ♥ bouquets for the bride and her attendants, corsages and buttonholes
- ♥ engagement and wedding rings
- ♥ presents for the attendants, best man and the ushers
- ♥ the first-night hotel
- ♥ the honeymoon

Wedding insurance A wedding should be a perfect day and you probably don't want to think about what you'd do if something went wrong. However, if you're spending large amounts of money on your celebrations, it's worth taking out insurance. There are various wedding policies on the market that offer cover for such things as damage to the wedding dress, theft of presents, loss of deposits if suppliers go bust and problems with photographs. Get several quotes and check very carefully to see what's included before you take out a policy.

Budget checklist	Estimated cost
Announcements	
Invitations, envelopes and postage	
Order of service sheets	
Other stationery (place cards, menus, cake boxes, etc.)	
total	
Dress	
Headdress	
Veil	
Jewellery	
Lingerie	
Shoes and hosiery	
Other accessories	
Hair and make-up	
total	
Men's formalwear hire	
Accessories: e.g. ties, cuff links, waistcoats	
Attendants' outfits, if you are paying for them	
total	
Bride's bouquet	
Bridesmaids' bouquets	
Buttonholes and corsages	
Flowers for the church or civil venue	
Flowers for the reception	
total	

Budget checklist	Estimated cost
Photographer	
Videographer	
total	
Church fees	
Civil ceremony fees	
Music for the ceremony	
total	
Reception venue	
Food	
Drink	
Cake	
Entertainment	
Favours and confetti	
Transport	
Insurance	
total	
Gifts: Attendants	
Best man	
Ushers	
Mothers	
total	
First-night hotel	
Honeymoon	
total	
total cost of the wedding	

notes

....
....
....
....
....
....
....
....
....
....
....
....
....
....
....
....
....
....
....
....
....
....
....
....
....
....
....
....
....
....

notes

....
....
....
....
....
....
....
....
....
....
....
....
....
....
....
....
....
....
....
....
....
....
....
....
....
....
....
....
....

Celebrating your engagement

The run-up to a wedding is a time of great excitement. You'll be thinking about the future, but don't forget to enjoy the present.

The ring The idea of a man getting down on bended knee and presenting his wife-to-be with a fabulous ring is very romantic. However, few grooms are sure enough of their fiancée's taste and ring size to risk this. With a piece of jewellery of this importance, it's probably best to make the choice together. By tradition, the groom buys the engagement and wedding ring (or rings) and is expected to spend about a month's salary on the former. However, this is only a guide, so spend what feels right, whether it's less or more. There's a huge choice of new rings on the market, or you could look at antique ones. You could even commission a jeweller to design and make a ring specially for you.

The classic engagement ring is a diamond solitaire, its popularity having much to do with the sparkle created by this type of cut (known as round or brilliant). For centuries diamonds have been associated with love and prized for their brilliance and exceptional hardness. However, there are other beautiful stones, including sapphires, rubies, emeralds and amethysts. Take your natural colouring – skin tone, hair and eyes – as your starting point when making your choice. Then think about the metal you'd like the stones set in (18-carat gold and platinum are very popular). There are many styles of setting, including prong (where tiny metal claws hold the stones); bezel (where a rim of metal

The symbolic significance of engagement and wedding rings, and their permanent place on your hand, make choosing them a big decision, so take your time.

Right and top centre Give your best man something to keep the rings safe in, such as a little box or bag, so that there are no awkward fumblings for them during the ceremony.

Above Wedding bands are often plain, but could be embellished with stones, patterns or engraving.

Top left Strong, sleek lines give these rings a modern, sophisticated look that's anything but traditional.

Top right A diamond solitaire is still the most popular setting for engagement rings.

surrounds them); cluster (where small stones surround a central one); and pavé (where almost no metal shows between the gems). Browse in a number of jewellers and try on lots of different styles. It's worth taking your time so you get the decision right. Since engagement and wedding rings are worn together, they should complement each other in terms of metal and gems used. Wedding bands are often plain, though they can be worked in some way, engraved (with your initials, marriage date or a sentiment) or set with stones.

♥ During the wedding ceremony, wear your engagement ring on the ring finger of your right hand. If it doesn't fit, give it to a bridesmaid or your mother for safe keeping. It should then go back on to your left hand, after your wedding ring.

Engagement parties Having an engagement party is a sociable way to get your wedding festivities going, but it's far from obligatory. If you're having a short engagement, you may feel that it's one thing too many to organize and that it will eat up money that you'd prefer to spend on the day itself. An engagement party is normally fairly small and intimate – certainly nowhere near the scale of a wedding reception – and held at the bride's home or that of her parents. It can

take any form, from drinks and nibbles to a buffet or seated meal. At some point during it, a formal announcement can be made of the couple's engagement in order to propose a toast to them. A few words may be said and there could be a cake. Since an engagement party is a more informal, smaller-scale event than a wedding, you may want to invite only immediate family and close friends. Think twice before you ask anyone who'll have to travel a distance, particularly if they'll be coming to the wedding. Another approach to an engagement party is to invite people who you won't be asking to the wedding itself, such as neighbours. Guests sometimes like to bring engagement presents, but this is an added bonus and not something to be expected.

Opposite and this page **An engagement party is an optional extra, but it's a nice excuse to gather together friends and relations. There may be people who haven't yet met your fiancé (or friends of his who haven't met you), and a party is also a way of including people in the celebrations who won't be invited to the wedding itself, such as neighbours. Don't feel that it's got to be a grand affair – you'll have enough on your plate with organizing the wedding, so keep things simple. There are no rules of etiquette to follow when planning your party, so how many people you invite and whether you offer drinks and canapés, a buffet or a sit-down meal is entirely up to you.**

Announcements You may want to announce your engagement in a local or national newspaper. Phone to check how much it will cost first. The usual wording is as follows:

> Mr D J Broadbent and Miss J F Porter
> The engagement is announced between David John, eldest son of Mr and Mrs Michael Broadbent of Woodstock, Oxfordshire, and Jane Frances, only daughter of Mr and Mrs Frederick Porter of Wilbury, West Sussex.

To avoid any mistakes, send or fax written details. If your or your fiancé's parents have divorced and/or remarried, the wording will have to be adapted (see pages 38 and 39 on the correct wording of invitations). If you're not sure, the newspaper should be able to advise you.

Hen parties

Hen parties have become more ambitious these days, and often last longer than an evening. The chief bridesmaid or another close friend normally organizes everything on the bride's behalf (and the bride is usually not expected to pay for anything herself). They may want to make it a surprise, but it's a good idea to let them know what you do and don't like and who you'd like to be there. Book a date as soon as possible so that everyone can keep it free and choose a practical location for the event that everyone will be able to get to easily. There are lots of possibilities, including a girls' get-together and delicious meal at someone's house; a pampering visit to a spa; a weekend house party at a country cottage; afternoon tea at a grand hotel; or a visit to the theatre or cinema with dinner in a restaurant to follow. However, keep the cost of the event within reasonable limits or some friends may feel that they can't afford to come.

Top and opposite left **A hen party is the perfect opportunity to spoil the bride with some indulgent presents – sybaritic bathtime treats, perhaps, or luxurious underwear.**

Right and opposite right **The hen night has mutated into a celebration which can take on any form, from a dinner party, as here, to a whole weekend away. You may even want to join forces with the groom and his friends. However, don't be so ambitious that the plans become a headache and don't lose sight of the key to the whole event: it's a chance to forget about the wedding preparations, relax in your friends' company and have a bit of fun.**

Above left **Providing favours is a nice way to make sure that everyone leaves with a memento of the occasion, whether it's a homemade cookie or something more permanent.**

Above right **Romantic rose table arrangements and hand-tied bunches of cutlery, all in shades of pink to match the china, make this celebration a special occasion.**

Stag parties These events have a bad reputation. We've all heard stories of hapless grooms waking up minus their trousers on the mail train to Inverness. While there will always be some grooms who think that a pub crawl with their friends the night before the wedding is a great idea, many take a more sophisticated approach and at the very least hold their bachelor celebrations well before the day. The event is usually organized by the best man (like the bride, the groom isn't expected to pay for his celebrations) and either he or another sensible friend should be given the task of making sure that the groom doesn't come to any

harm if things get out of hand. Stag parties are what stag nights have become, reflecting the fact that, like hen parties, they're often not just one evening but a whole day or even a weekend. Alcohol is bound to play a significant role in the average stag party but outdoor activities or sports, such as golf, clay-pigeon shooting or go-karting, have become a very popular way for the stags to spend time together, and they are a good way to create group atmosphere. However, it's easy for the event to become expensive and it's a shame if anyone feels excluded or under pressure to spend more than they can afford.

notes

notes

....
....
....
....
....
....
....
....
....
....
....
....
....
....
....
....
....
....
....
....
....
....
....
....
....
....
....

Mr. and Mrs. Christopher
request the pleasure of
your company at the marr
of their daughter
Jennifer
to
Mr Robin Bi
at the Church of St. Fra
on Saturday 1st Ma
at 3 o'clock
and afterwards at
14 Birdcage Walk, sw

Road
on SW10 0QJ

Invitations and stationery

Wedding stationery has a decorative as well as a practical purpose and can be used creatively to reflect your taste and style.

Invitations If you're having a small wedding, you could hand write your invitations. For larger numbers, printing is more practical. If money's tight and you're good on the computer or have an artistic friend, you may be able to produce something yourself. Stationery in high-street shops is good value.

Traditional invitations are printed in black on white or cream card and may be hand engraved (the most expensive option), thermographed (designed to look like hand engraving, but cheaper) or flat printed (the cheapest method). Check proofs very carefully before okaying them for printing. Traditional wordings are given on page 39, but there's no reason why you shouldn't have something less formal if it suits the mood of your wedding. With formal invitations, guests' names are handwritten in the top left corner or the space provided in the wording of the invitation, and full titles are used. If you're sending an invitation to a married couple, the correct form of address on the envelope is 'Mr and Mrs Joseph Bloggs'; if it's to a family, 'Mr and Mrs Joseph Bloggs, Paul and Elizabeth'. It's traditional to send an invitation to your groom's parents and, if you're having a church wedding, to the minister (and spouse if married). If your reception includes a formal dinner and dance and you want guests to wear black tie and evening dress, 'Black Tie' should be printed in the bottom right corner of your invitations. If you're having an evening party to which you're inviting extra guests, there should be a separate invitation for this. It's not considered appropriate to stipulate morning dress on invitations since this could put your guests to inconvenience and expense. Send invitations out two or three months before the day to be safe and certainly no later than six weeks before. Don't forget to enclose maps and accommodation information if necessary.

Far left and below **Ask your stationer or printer for samples showing different styles of typeface. Traditional invitations are printed with words alone, but there's nothing to stop you choosing ones with motifs, illustrations or photographs.**

Above centre and right **Place cards give lots of scope for ingenuity and creativity. Here, they've been placed in pretty teacups and tucked into folded napkins. Place cards are often written rather than printed for a personal touch. If your writing isn't neat enough, you could use a professional calligrapher.**

Wordings for invitations Opposite are some standard wordings for wedding invitations. If you're hosting your own wedding, begin 'Jane Porter and David Broadbent request the pleasure of your company at their marriage…

Other items of wedding stationery

Reply cards You don't have to include pre-printed reply cards with your invitations, though they may encourage your guests to reply more promptly.

Thank-yous Since your guests have gone to the trouble of buying you a gift, you should take the trouble of handwriting a personal thank-you. Try to tackle them as presents arrive.

Orders of service Couples often print these for church weddings and blessings. Inside, details of the music and readings, the order of the service and the hymns are printed to make it easy for everyone to follow. Establish what form of service you're having with your minister before you contact the printer.

Place cards If you're having a seating plan at your reception, you'll need place cards of some sort for the tables. These can be printed or handwritten (for more ideas, see page 107).

Menus These are optional. You could have a small menu per guest (which could be taken away as a memento) or a larger one for each table. Your hotel or caterer may be able to supply them, so ask before you order printed ones.

Table plans You'll need one of these if you're having a seated meal, well displayed so all your guests can easily see where to go (see page 104).

Table stationery You may want to go the whole hog and order coasters, napkins, napkin rings, match books and so on with your names or initials and the date of your wedding. However, make sure that more important things such as food and drink are adequately covered in your budget first.

Calligraphers If your writing isn't as elegant as you'd like and you want to give your stationery a flourish, calligraphers can be hired to write invitations, place cards, table plans, menus and so on. Ask for samples of different styles.

♥ To make a keepsake that you can pore over when you're back from honeymoon, provide a message book for your guests to sign. Place in a prominent position at the reception or ask one of your ushers to circulate it.

Opposite **Wordings for invitations, clockwise from top left: invitation to a wedding, bride's parents as hosts; invitation to a wedding, bride's parents as hosts (alternative wording); invitation to a wedding, bride's parents divorced and mother remarried (if mother is not remarried, begin 'Mr Frederick Porter and Mrs Judy Porter'); invitation to a civil wedding at a licensed venue; invitation to an evening party; invitation to a service of blessing; invitation to a wedding reception only.**

Below **If you're having an evening party after the first part of your reception and want to invite extra guests, separate invitations can be printed on single cards.**

Mr and Mrs Frederick Porter
request the pleasure of
your company at the marriage
of their daughter
Jane Frances
to
Mr David Broadbent
at St Michael's Church, Wilbury,
on Saturday, 25th July 2001
at 3pm
and afterwards at
The White Swan Hotel, Wilbury

RSVP
[Address]

Mr and Mrs Frederick Porter
request the pleasure of the company of
[name of guest(s) written by hand]
at the marriage of their daughter
Jane Frances...

Mr Frederick Porter and Mrs James Culver
request the pleasure of
your company at the marriage
of their daughter
Jane Frances...

Mr and Mrs Frederick Porter
request the pleasure of
your company at a reception
following the marriage
of their daughter
Jane Frances
to
Mr David Broadbent
at...

Mr and Mrs Frederick Porter
request the pleasure of
your company at the marriage
of their daughter
Jane Frances
to
Mr David Broadbent
at The White Swan Hotel, Wilbury,
on Saturday, 25th July 2001
at 3pm
followed by a reception

Mr and Mrs Frederick Porter
request the pleasure of
your company
at the blessing of the marriage
of their daughter
Jane Frances
to...

Mr and Mrs Frederick Porter
request the pleasure of
your company at an evening party
to celebrate the marriage
of their daughter
Jane Frances
to...

notes

....
....
....
....
....
....
....
....
....
....
....
....
....
....
....
....
....
....
....
....
....
....
....
....
....
....
....
....

notes

....
....
....
....
....
....
....
....
....
....
....
....
....
....
....
....
....
....
....
....
....
....
....
....
....
....
....
....
....
....

The guests

Sharing your day with friends and family, whether it's a select few or a small army of them, will heighten the joy of your celebrations.

The guest list

The guest list The size of your guest list is dictated by your budget. If you've set your heart on a certain venue, this may also limit numbers. Once you've set a maximum head count, don't be tempted to exceed it. It's vital not to overstretch yourselves financially – nothing will sour your celebrations more quickly than finding that bills can't be met or that cutbacks have to be made in other areas of your wedding. Don't rely on a drop-out rate, either, because you'll be in trouble if all your guests accept. Remember that going to a wedding can be expensive for guests and that entertaining them well is the main function of a reception. It's not fair to invite a small army of people and then expect them to make do with a few nibbles. Moreover, don't invite so many guests that you won't be able to speak, at least briefly, to all of them during the day.

The easiest way to draw up a list is to start by including everyone you'd ideally like to invite, then start eliminating. This is often a difficult process, but think, for instance, about crossing off people you haven't seen for several years. You're also not obliged to invite colleagues from work or to include an escort for single friends. Most couples draw up their guest list with their parents. Even if the couple themselves or the bride's parents are footing the whole bill, it's only fair that everyone has a chance to say whom they'd like to invite. Deciding how to share out the list between the different parties demands diplomacy if you're to avoid giving offence. Make this one of the first things you sort out so that everyone knows where they stand. Things can become difficult if parents feel that their share of the guest list should be larger than the bride and groom

Above left and centre **Weddings are sociable occasions and most guests make the most of the opportunity to dress up. Hats were once a must for women but sartorial codes have relaxed and whether or not to wear one is now a matter of personal choice.**

Above right **For male guests, morning dress is the traditional option. However, few men nowadays have it in their wardrobes, so any smart form of dress is just as acceptable. Guests should not feel pressurized into hiring or buying formalwear, so morning dress should never be stipulated on invitations.**

would like. For instance, there may be distant relatives whom they want to invite for etiquette's sake; you may want to invite more of your friends. Some couples have a two-tiered reception, inviting a small group of guests to the ceremony and meal, then having an evening party to which additional guests are invited. The final list will inevitably be the result of negotiation and compromise. But remember that if you invite someone to your celebrations, it should be because you really want them to be there, so you and your fiancé should have the final say. When you've completed your guest list, you could send out 'save the date' cards well ahead of your invitations.

Inviting children Whether or not to invite children is a tricky decision. Start by working out how many there would be if all your guests brought their families. If you decide not to include children, it's diplomatic to let people know verbally so that you can explain your reasons and avoid causing upset. You'll also have to accept that some guests won't be able to arrange for their children to be looked after during your wedding and therefore won't be able to come. Whatever you decide, it has to be one decision that goes for all. The only exception to this is your immediate family – it's natural to invite little nieces and nephews even if you're not having any other children. If you do include children, think about ways to keep them happy. If there are lots of them, you could look into hiring an entertainer or a bouncy castle. A special children's table at the reception is a good idea, complete with crayons and paper or toys to keep them amused, and child-friendly food. There are also companies which provide crèche services for weddings.

Seating guests It is the ushers' job to show guests to their seats as they arrive for the ceremony. For a church wedding, the groom's family and guests are traditionally seated to the right of the aisle, and the bride's to the left, with key family members in the front seats. However, many guests will be mutual friends, so ushers should simply ensure that there's a balance of people on each side. The bride's mother and groom's parents sit at the front of the church (if there's a chief usher, he or she should show them to their seats). Even if parents are divorced, it's the norm for them to sit together for the service.

Opposite top left Remember that guests will begin arriving well before the ceremony, so make sure that your ushers do, too, so that everyone can be shown to their seats.

Opposite top right If you're providing orders of service, give someone the responsibility of handing them out as guests arrive for the ceremony.

Opposite below left If you're going to invite guests from abroad, let them know the date of your wedding as soon as possible so that they have plenty of time to make travel arrangements.

Opposite below right Men's wedding formalwear now comes in many guises, from frock coats to traditional Highland dress.

Below Making your guests feel welcome is the key to a successful reception. If you're having a receiving line, it's a nice idea to offer everyone drinks as they wait.

Guests

Address

RSVP   No. in party

Gift   Thank-you

Guests

Address

RSVP   No. in party

Gift   Thank-you

Guests

Address

RSVP   No. in party

Gift   Thank-you

Guests

Address

RSVP   No. in party

Gift   Thank-you

Guests

Address

RSVP   No. in party

Gift   Thank-you

Guests

Address

RSVP   No. in party

Gift   Thank-you

Guests

Address

RSVP   No. in party

Gift   Thank-you

Guests

Address

RSVP   No. in party

Gift   Thank-you

Guests			Guests		
Address			Address		
RSVP		No. in party	RSVP		No. in party
Gift		Thank-you	Gift		Thank-you

Guests			Guests		
Address			Address		
RSVP		No. in party	RSVP		No. in party
Gift		Thank-you	Gift		Thank-you

Guests			Guests		
Address			Address		
RSVP		No. in party	RSVP		No. in party
Gift		Thank-you	Gift		Thank-you

Guests			Guests		
Address			Address		
RSVP		No. in party	RSVP		No. in party
Gift		Thank-you	Gift		Thank-you

Guests			Guests		
Address			Address		
RSVP		No. in party	RSVP		No. in party
Gift		Thank-you	Gift		Thank-you

Guests			Guests		
Address			Address		
RSVP		No. in party	RSVP		No. in party
Gift		Thank-you	Gift		Thank-you

Guests			Guests		
Address			Address		
RSVP	No. in party		RSVP	No. in party	
Gift	Thank-you		Gift	Thank-you	
Guests			Guests		
Address			Address		
RSVP	No. in party		RSVP	No. in party	
Gift	Thank-you		Gift	Thank-you	
Guests			Guests		
Address			Address		
RSVP	No. in party		RSVP	No. in party	
Gift	Thank-you		Gift	Thank-you	
Guests			Guests		
Address			Address		
RSVP	No. in party		RSVP	No. in party	
Gift	Thank-you		Gift	Thank-you	
Guests			Guests		
Address			Address		
RSVP	No. in party		RSVP	No. in party	
Gift	Thank-you		Gift	Thank-you	
Guests			Guests		
Address			Address		
RSVP	No. in party		RSVP	No. in party	
Gift	Thank-you		Gift	Thank-you	

Guests
....
Address
....

....
RSVP .... No. in party ....
Gift .... Thank-you ....

Guests
....
Address
....

....
RSVP .... No. in party ....
Gift .... Thank-you ....

Guests
....
Address
....

....
RSVP .... No. in party ....
Gift .... Thank-you ....

Guests
....
Address
....

....
RSVP .... No. in party ....
Gift .... Thank-you ....

Guests
....
Address
....

....
RSVP .... No. in party ....
Gift .... Thank-you ....

Guests
....
Address
....

....
RSVP .... No. in party ....
Gift .... Thank-you ....

Guests
....
Address
....

....
RSVP .... No. in party ....
Gift .... Thank-you ....

Guests
....
Address
....

....
RSVP .... No. in party ....
Gift .... Thank-you ....

Guests
....
Address
....

....
RSVP .... No. in party ....
Gift .... Thank-you ....

Guests
....
Address
....

....
RSVP .... No. in party ....
Gift .... Thank-you ....

Guests
....
Address
....

....
RSVP .... No. in party ....
Gift .... Thank-you ....

Guests
....
Address
....

....
RSVP .... No. in party ....
Gift .... Thank-you ....

Guests

Address

RSVP   No. in party

Gift   Thank-you

Guests

Address

RSVP   No. in party

Gift   Thank-you

Guests

Address

RSVP   No. in party

Gift   Thank-you

Guests

Address

RSVP   No. in party

Gift   Thank-you

Guests

Address

RSVP   No. in party

Gift   Thank-you

Guests

Address

RSVP   No. in party

Gift   Thank-you

Guests

Address

RSVP   No. in party

Gift   Thank-you

Guests

Address

RSVP   No. in party

Gift   Thank-you

Guests

Address

RSVP   No. in party

Gift   Thank-you

Guests

Address

RSVP   No. in party

Gift   Thank-you

Guests

Address

RSVP   No. in party

Gift   Thank-you

Guests

Address

RSVP   No. in party

Gift   Thank-you

Guests	Guests
Address	Address
RSVP	No. in party	RSVP	No. in party
Gift	Thank-you	Gift	Thank-you

Guests

Address

RSVP   No. in party

Gift   Thank-you

Guests

Address

RSVP   No. in party

Gift   Thank-you

Guests

Address

RSVP   No. in party

Gift   Thank-you

Guests

Address

RSVP   No. in party

Gift   Thank-you

Guests

Address

RSVP   No. in party

Gift   Thank-you

Guests
Address

RSVP   No. in party
Gift   Thank-you

Guests
Address

RSVP   No. in party
Gift   Thank-you

Guests
Address

RSVP   No. in party
Gift   Thank-you

Guests
Address

RSVP   No. in party
Gift   Thank-you

Guests
Address

RSVP   No. in party
Gift   Thank-you

Guests
Address

RSVP   No. in party
Gift   Thank-you

Guests
Address

RSVP   No. in party
Gift   Thank-you

Guests
Address

RSVP   No. in party
Gift   Thank-you

Guests
Address

RSVP   No. in party
Gift   Thank-you

Guests
Address

RSVP   No. in party
Gift   Thank-you

Guests
Address

RSVP   No. in party
Gift   Thank-you

Guests
Address

RSVP   No. in party
Gift   Thank-you

Guests		Guests	
Address		Address	
RSVP	No. in party	RSVP	No. in party
Gift	Thank-you	Gift	Thank-you

Guests		Guests	
Address		Address	
RSVP	No. in party	RSVP	No. in party
Gift	Thank-you	Gift	Thank-you

Guests		Guests	
Address		Address	
RSVP	No. in party	RSVP	No. in party
Gift	Thank-you	Gift	Thank-you

Guests		Guests	
Address		Address	
RSVP	No. in party	RSVP	No. in party
Gift	Thank-you	Gift	Thank-you

Guests		Guests	
Address		Address	
RSVP	No. in party	RSVP	No. in party
Gift	Thank-you	Gift	Thank-you

Guests		Guests	
Address		Address	
RSVP	No. in party	RSVP	No. in party
Gift	Thank-you	Gift	Thank-you

The bridal party

The bride and groom are the stars of the day but their best man,
attendants and ushers play special supporting roles.

The parents of young attendants are traditionally expected to pay for their outfits, but many brides choose to make a gift of the clothes, particularly if they're expensive or unlikely to be worn again.

Left and below **A fairy-tale dress is guaranteed to make this little flower girl feel like a princess for the day. The dress is classic in style, with a fitted bodice and full, filmy skirts. Ballet shoes finish the outfit, below. Your bridesmaids' outfits should echo and emphasize the day's style or theme. Here, butterfly motifs and subtle shades of mauve and lilac complement the bride's bouquet and the wedding's summery mood.**

The helpers Whether or not you have attendants and ushers is a matter of personal choice. If you're having a register office wedding, you're unlikely to need ushers for the ceremony. It's usual to have a best man, but you could have two, and the best man could be a best woman. There's a lot to think about when you're organizing a wedding, so make use of your chief bridesmaid and best man if you need extra help before the day.

Attendants The bride may want to have a chief bridesmaid (she's called this if she's single, matron of honour if she's married). The chief bridesmaid is the bride's right-hand woman on the day, so she should be well-organized and practical. If there isn't a chief bridesmaid, parcel out her duties (see next page) among your adult bridesmaids. There's no doubt that young bridesmaids (also known as flower girls) and pageboys add great charm to a wedding, but it can be a long and tiring day for them. Have at least one adult bridesmaid to supervise them, and seat parents within sight of their children during the ceremony for reassurance. Make sure you know where the nearest toilet is in case of emergencies and give children a toy to occupy them. It's a shame if the marriage itself is disrupted by noisy children, so someone should be ready to take them outside for a play if they become fractious. The best man is the groom's chief helper, and has a fairly long list of duties (see page 70) and a speech to make. He also needs to be organized and calm.

Above **Older pageboys may prefer a more adult style of outfit to the classic sailor suit or knickerbockers – here, a striped, collarless jacket with striking buttonhole. You may also want to give one pageboy the job of being your ring bearer and carrying the rings up the aisle on a special cushion.**

Below **A great deal of attention to detail has gone into this bridesmaid's outfit. The same romantic palette of lilacs and mauves has been used for the dress and flowers, and the fabric butterflies in her hair pick up the fluttering organza motifs on the dress.**

The chief bridesmaid's duties are:

- ♥ to organize the hen party;
- ♥ to help the bride choose her dress and the attendants' outfits;
- ♥ to help the bride get ready before the wedding;
- ♥ to make sure that the bride's honeymoon luggage is sent to the reception venue or on to the hotel;
- ♥ to wait for the bride to arrive outside the ceremony venue and keep an eye on young attendants;
- ♥ to arrange the bride's veil and train before she walks up the aisle;
- ♥ to take the bride's bouquet when she gets to the top of the aisle and look after it during the ceremony. At a church wedding, she takes it into the vestry for the signing of the register. She returns the bouquet to the bride for the walk back down the aisle.
- ♥ to look after the bride's dress once she's changed into her going-away outfit.

Attendants' outfits The question of who pays for the attendants' outfits can be an awkward one, since it's traditionally down to the parents of young attendants or adult bridesmaids themselves, not the bride or her parents. It's important to get things clear from the start, but be sensitive. Parents have a great many other things to spend their money on and may balk at the idea of expensive clothes that their children will wear only once. If you've set your heart on pricey outfits, you should be prepared to pay for them yourself.

If your adult bridesmaids are paying for their own outfits, involve them in choosing them so that they end up with something they'll want to wear again. Few women are thrilled by the thought of walking down the aisle looking like an oversized fairy and are far more likely to want something sophisticated and glamorous. Eveningwear is often a good place to start looking. If you don't want your adult bridesmaids to be dressed identically, you could have dresses made from the same fabric but allow your bridesmaids to choose their own style.

With young bridesmaids, the choice of clothes is easier as little girls look charming in any sort of pretty dress and will probably be only too happy to look like fairies or princesses. Remember that unless they're very young, boys may not be keen on knickerbockers and frilly shirts or sailor suits. Smart trousers and a shirt or even miniature morning dress may be a better idea. If you have a number of young attendants, give

someone the responsibility of looking after them on the morning of the wedding, such as your chief bridesmaid. It's important for you to have time to yourself when you're getting ready. Ideally, ask their parents to dress their children to help to keep them calm, and leave this until as late as possible to keep clothes clean.

♥ Furnishing fabrics and brocades are ideal if you're having pageboys' waistcoats made, and are often cheaper than dress fabrics. You could coordinate pageboys, groom and best man in matching waistcoats.

♥ If you're buying off-the-peg bridesmaids' dresses, customize them by adding sashes to match your colour scheme, or sew on fabric flowers or bows.

♥ Some brides like to have a ring bearer, a pageboy who walks up the aisle with the other attendants with the rings on a small cushion.

The mothers One of the most flattering fashion options for the mother of the bride or the groom is a suit, whether a jacket and skirt, jacket and dress or jacket and smart trousers. If there is an evening reception, choose a fabric that will help to make the transition from wedding to party, such as silk or brocade. Colour should take its cue from the bride and tone in with her scheme; traditionally, mothers should not wear white or off-white. Though hats aren't mandatory, most mothers relish the opportunity to wear one. A corsage is another optional extra but is a nice way of marking the mothers out.

Gifts It's usual for the bride and groom to present gifts to the attendants, the best man and their mothers at the wedding. These don't have to be extravagant, simply something that the recipients will be able to keep as reminders of the day. Jewellery is popular for mothers and adult bridesmaids. For young attendants, a toy to play with on the day is a good ploy. It's a nice gesture to present the mothers with their presents or bouquets of flowers during the groom's speech at the reception as a way of publicly acknowledging their help.

The dress Buying a beautiful dress that will only be worn once is a grand gesture unique to weddings, and choosing this all-important creation is a big moment for any bride. And though 'wedding' and 'dress' always go together, your dream outfit may be a satin coat, a short shift or a trousersuit. Whatever you buy, make sure it's something that you feel relaxed, comfortable and confident in.

Buying a dress Brides come in all shapes and sizes and so do wedding dresses, but finding the right match isn't always easy. You're lucky if you know exactly what sort of dress suits you. If you don't, keep an open mind when you visit shops, and try on lots of different styles. A dress that looks unpromising on the hanger may be transformed once you've put it on. Wedding dresses can be bought off the peg or ready to wear, meaning that they've been manufactured to a standard size. A made-to-measure dress is usually a pre-existing design that is made to your measurements. With a couture dress, the designer starts from scratch, creating a one-off garment for the client. An off-the-peg dress is the least expensive option. If you're having a made-to-measure or couture dress, allow four months or more for it to be made.

When you go to look for a dress, take along someone whose opinion you trust for moral support and an objective view. Wear your wedding underwear to your fittings and try on a veil, headdress and shoes to get an idea of the finished look. In particular, make sure that the bodice of your dress fits well: people's eyes will be on your face, which means that the top half of your dress will also come under close scrutiny.

Dress styles

♥ Ballgown or ballerina-style dress with a fitted top and full skirt: best avoided if you're short, but good if you've got a large bust or hips, or are pear-shaped, because it defines the waist and balances the top and bottom halves of the body. If you've got a round tummy, try a flat-fronted fitted bodice that goes into a V-shape at the waist. With a large bust, avoid fussy bows or ruffles at the neckline; a simple scoop is better.

♥ Column or bias-cut dress: great if you're slim (whether tall or small). Not out of the question for larger women, but you need to be well-proportioned and not top or bottom heavy.

♥ Empire-line dress: a good choice if you're short and if you're pear-shaped or full-figured as it 'skims' the body, disguising large hips.

♥ Princess-line dress (fitted bodice and A-line skirt but no seam at the waist): flatters pear-shaped figures, thick waists, big hips and heavy legs. A good choice for small women since it doesn't have a waistline that 'cuts' the body in half.

Opposite and below
A strapless or sleeveless wedding dress is a sophisticated choice and looks suitably glamorous at an evening reception. However, it could leave you feeling a little exposed during the ceremony, particularly if it is being held in church. A stylish solution is to wear with it a coat, jacket or wrap made from a diaphanous fabric such as chiffon or organza.

Fabrics These are often available in both silk and synthetic forms. Silk feels and looks wonderful, but synthetics often crease less. Duchesse satin, particularly the silk variety, has a glorious lustre and its weight forms beautiful folds. Raw, dupion, shantung and Thai silks are popular wedding fabrics. Crêpe is fine and fluid, making it ideal for slim-cut dresses. Sheer fabrics such as organza and tulle look wonderful made into filmy overskirts or lightweight jackets, coats or wraps. Stiffer fabrics, such as zibeline and mikado, are popular for modern, structured designs. The rich and soft look of velvet makes it ideal for winter dresses.

Colours Pure white is quintessentially bridal but can be draining to pale skins. Off-white, ivory and cream shades are more flattering. Gold or peach is good with golden or creamy skin and warm or reddish hair colours, as well as black and Asian skins. Silver suits olive skin tones and black hair, or ash-blond to dark blond hair and blue-green or grey-blue eyes. Pale blue, peach, lilac and pink are good with fair hair and skin or as a dramatic contrast to dark hair and eyes.

Saving money Many manufacturers produce affordable, stylish wedding dresses. Synthetic fabrics are cheaper than silks, and column styles are less expensive than full ones because they use less fabric. You could hire a dress or buy one second-hand (it will only have been worn for a few hours). Look out for sales at bridal shops. Having a dress made is often cheaper than buying one, but you must have total confidence in your dressmaker. You could consider wearing your mother's wedding dress – vintage styles often look just as chic today.

Above left **Black tie is one option for an evening reception. This bride has chosen a gown whose sleek, sophisticated lines take it into the realm of eveningwear.**

Above right **Slim, column dresses are very popular with modern brides but can show every bulge. Fitted bodices and full skirts are more forgiving if you've got a generous bust or hips. Try on plenty of styles to find the one that's most flattering.**

Opposite **Stark white can be hard to wear – ivory or cream is more flattering for most colourings.**

Looking after your dress Have your dress professionally dry-cleaned straight after your honeymoon, before stains become ingrained. Read the care label, and if you have any worries call the manufacturer. Remove fabric-covered metal buttons. Store your dress in a box lined with acid-free tissue paper, not a PVC cover, and stuff the bodice and sleeves with tissue to preserve their shape. Lavender sachets will help to keep moths out. Then put the box in a cool, dark, dry cupboard.

♥ If you're wearing high heels, remember they easily tear fine fabric.

♥ If paper confetti gets wet it can stain, so brush it off your dress.

♥ Champagne spills can turn into brown stains after dry-cleaning, so sponge them off.

♥ Lily pollen stains, so remove stamens if you choose these flowers.

Lingerie Good-quality underwear is a worthwhile investment. Wear your wedding underwear when trying on dresses and for fittings. A well-fitting bra is vital, so visit a shop where they will measure you properly. Designers often sew little clips into the necklines of wedding dresses to keep bras in place. Wash bras in lukewarm water and don't tumble-dry or put on the radiator – bras hate heat. With slim styles of dress in fine fabrics, wear smooth, seamless underwear in white, ivory or nude shades to give you a good line, and avoid suspender belts and stockings. Pants or tights with control panels over the tummy are also useful. You can wear most things under a full dress in a heavier fabric, including lacy or embroidered underwear.

Accessories

Veils The veil is traditionally worn over the face until the exchange of vows. Many brides now prefer to wear it back, framing the face. Visit your hairdresser a couple of months before your wedding for a practice session with your veil and headdress. Even if your veil is attached to a comb, use hairgrips. For extra hold, use two at a time, sliding one over the other to make a cross.

Lengths A long veil which forms a train is known as cathedral length and looks best with a long, traditional dress. A shoulder- or waist-length veil works with most styles of dress. A full veil can make a round face look wider but gives a softer look to a long face, while a straight veil helps to slim a wide face.

Colours Usually white or cream, veils are also available in pastels and metallics.

Fabrics Lace is the classic choice. Antique lace is exquisite, though you could try soaking new lace in cold tea to give an aged effect. Synthetic net and tulle are popular and give a stiffer, more structured look that suits modern dresses. Many have embellishments such as pearls, beads, sequins, embroidery and shaped or trimmed edges. Real silk tulle is expensive, but hangs beautifully. If you can't find a veil you like, you could buy tulle, chiffon or organza and make your own.

Headdresses A tiara is traditional, though few brides are lucky enough to have a family heirloom to wear. However, there are tiaras, coronets and crowns available in affordable materials, many of them decorated with beads, crystals and pearls. One word of warning: crowns and coronets need lots of pins to make them secure. If you want something smaller, try decorated hairgrips, slides, combs or Alice bands. Real flowers look pretty made into a circlet or pinned individually in the hair. Fabric flowers are a good alternative and are guaranteed not to wilt. Feathers give a sophisticated and dramatic look, as do hats, a good choice for brides wanting to get away from traditional headdresses.

Shoes You're going to be on your feet for a long time, so comfort is essential. High heels help to make legs look longer, though a lower, kitten heel has a similar effect. Column dresses need a heel; a ballgown style works well with a low heel or pumps. Wear your shoes in around the house. Take them to your dress fittings for adjustments to the hem. If they've got smooth soles, roughen them with sandpaper or score with scissors, to prevent slipping. If you buy white satin or silk shoes, they can be dyed afterwards for you to wear again.

Very white tights or stockings can make legs look anaemic; nude-coloured ones are more flattering. Give someone a spare pair to keep handy, in case you get a ladder. Though they don't have a practical purpose, decorative garters are still popular and are a way to add 'something blue' to your ensemble.

Other accessories

♥ A tiny bag can be useful for lipstick, powder and scent, or it may be possible to have a pocket sewn into the seam of your dress.

♥ Some brides like to carry lucky horseshoes, Bibles or decorative fans as well as their bouquet.

♥ Gloves are not as popular as they once were. Keep them on as you come down the aisle, with your engagement ring underneath on your right hand. At the top of the aisle, remove them and give them to your chief bridesmaid. You can put them on again if you wish after signing the register and wear them at the reception for welcoming guests, removing them for the meal.

Opposite top **Veils and headdresses can be difficult to fix in place yourself, so enlist the help of a hairdresser or bridesmaid. Have a trial run before the day and make sure you've got lots of grips and hairspray.**

Opposite centre **A little bag can be useful for keeping powder, lipstick, scent and a tissue or two handy.**

Opposite below and below **Wedding shoes must feel as comfortable as they look beautiful, since you'll be on your feet for much of the day and may be dancing. Wear them in around the house for a week or so before the wedding.**

Beauty Every bride wants to look radiant, but now isn't the time to transform your image. Just be yourself, but be your best self.

Diet and shape The months before a wedding are not a time for crash diets. Sudden weight loss can make dress fittings difficult. Focus instead on lifestyle changes that will produce health benefits for years to come. Eat healthily and exercise for half an hour three times a week (start gently if you've not done much before). Watch your caffeine intake and drink eight glasses of water a day.

Face The first step to good skin is thorough cleansing. A rinse- or wipe-off emulsion suits most skin types. Exfoliating once a week with a gentle scrub and using a mask can also help to keep your complexion clear. Avoid alcohol-based toners; use something gentler or try rosewater from the chemist. On honeymoon, protect your skin with an SPF at least 15 (look for high UVA and UVB protection); at home, wear a moisturizer with sunscreen every day (and don't forget your neck). Kick-start your regime with a professional facial, though not the week before your wedding, in case of temporary break-outs.

Hair Use a gentle shampoo as often as your hair needs it. Massage your scalp gently as you lather it up, to stimulate circulation and relieve stress. Rinse thoroughly with cool water for the final rinse, to encourage the hair's cuticles to lie flat, making it look shiny. Try a weekly deep-conditioning treatment and have regular trims to avoid split ends. If you're wearing your hair up, avoid washing it on the wedding morning, as this can make it 'slippery' and hard to handle. Start thinking about your wedding hairstyle well before the day. Don't go for a dramatic change unless you're absolutely sure it'll work.

Make-up Unless you're very expert with cosmetics, aim for a natural look using neutral colours. You'll get away with slightly stronger colours if you are getting married in the evening or winter. The shades that suit most colourings are creams, beiges, browns and greys for the eyes, and pinky-brown, rosy and tawny shades for cheeks and lips. If you wear little or no make-up normally, keep things very light. Visit a department store and see which cosmetics companies offer make-up lessons. Practise before the day so you feel confident.

Scent Perfumed products can damage fabrics, so apply perfume well before you dress to give it time to dry. Perfume itself, or parfum, is the most concentrated form of scent, followed by eau de parfum and eau de toilette. You may want to have a purse-size scent bottle with you for reapplications during the day. Scent is best applied to the inside of the elbow and wrist, the dip of the collarbone and navel. Avoid behind your ears – secretions from sebaceous glands here can alter a scent's smell.

Opposite A bride's hair should be her crowning glory. Have at least one trial run with your hairdresser well before the day so you can be sure that the style will work.

Below A bride's hands come under a lot of scrutiny, so get them into good shape by using hand cream regularly and massaging it into your cuticles. File nails in one direction to avoid damaging the nail plate. A professional manicure is a nice pre-wedding treat and will help to form good habits. If you're going to varnish your nails, do it the night before the wedding to give the nails plenty of time to dry.

The groom Morning dress is the traditional choice for the groom: a black morning coat; fawn waistcoat; white shirt; and grey-and-black-striped trousers. A grey coat, waistcoat and trouser suit is a variation. Top hats are optional and invariably end up being carried rather than worn. Most grooms hire their formalwear, though many hire shops sell off ex-hire clothes at good prices. A less formal choice is a suit – from cream linen for summer, to navy or dark grey wool for winter. If your groom wants something more flamboyant, embroidered silk or velvet frock coats and Nehru jackets are popular. Colour and pattern can be added to any outfit with ties, cuff links and waistcoats. For a wedding followed by an evening reception or dinner dance, black tie is an option (if you choose this, print 'Black Tie' on your invitations). However, it is not considered correct to specify morning dress on invitations, since this puts your guests to the trouble and expense of hiring it. Spread the word verbally if you really want to, but don't make anyone feel awkward. Whatever your groom wears, the male members of the bridal party should dress similarly.

The best man The best man is the groom's chief helper, keeping an eye on things on the day. **The best man's duties are:**

- ♥ to keep up-to-date with all the arrangements;
- ♥ to arrange the stag party and make sure that the groom gets home safely;
- ♥ to help organize outfits for himself, the groom and the ushers and to make sure they're collected;
- ♥ to help the groom to get ready on the day and ensure he arrives for the ceremony in good time;
- ♥ to coordinate the ushers and make sure they know what their duties are;
- ♥ to check that the buttonholes arrive and that the orders of service are ready to be handed out;
- ♥ to make sure that the groom's going-away clothes are at the reception venue;
- ♥ to make sure that any fees (such as organist and choir) payable on the day are settled;
- ♥ to look after the ring(s) and hand them to the minister or groom during the ceremony;
- ♥ to help to get guests together for photographs;
- ♥ to make sure that the ushers organize lifts to the reception for anyone who needs them;

♥ to escort the bride and groom to their car to go to the reception and to escort the bridesmaids to the reception;

♥ to announce the speeches and the cake-cutting, if there is no toastmaster;

♥ to read out cards or messages at the reception, and make the final speech;

♥ to look after the groom's clothes once he's changed, and return hired items;

♥ to announce the bride and groom's departure from the reception and to make sure that their luggage has been packed or sent on to their hotel.

Ushers
Ushers (male or female) are friends or relatives of the groom and have a useful role to play at any wedding, helping everything to run smoothly.

The ushers' duties are:

♥ to be at the venue well before the wedding, to hand out orders of service as guests arrive and to show them to their seats;

♥ to escort the bride's mother and groom's parents to their seats at the front of the church (if there is one, the chief usher should do this);

♥ to tell guests where to park, and have umbrellas to hand if it's raining;

♥ to be ready to seat latecomers;

♥ to help to get guests together for formal photographs;

♥ to help the best man organize lifts for guests to the reception, if necessary;

♥ to make sure that everyone has found their seats at the reception.

Opposite left **Black tie is a formalwear option if your wedding is being followed by an evening reception.**

Opposite right **It's up to you how many ushers you have and whether you have a chief usher to supervise the others.**

Right **The best man has the most demanding role in the wedding party, since he's the groom's right-hand man and is meant to keep a general eye on the smooth running of events. He acts as master of ceremonies in the absence of a toastmaster and, of course, is expected to deliver an amusing speech.**

Far right **It's usual to provide buttonholes for all the men in the bridal party. Make sure that whoever receives them on the morning of the wedding counts them to check that there are enough.**

notes

notes

The wedding day

Whether you exchange vows in a church, licensed venue or
register office, the marriage ceremony is at the heart of the day.
Then the celebrations can begin ...

The venue You may need a venue for a reception after a wedding, or a licensed venue in which to hold both civil ceremony and reception.

Types of venue If you or your parents have a large garden, you could have the reception at home in a marquee and hire a caterer. Hotels and restaurants can usually take care of all the arrangements, down to cake and flowers, which is useful if you're short of time. Other options are church halls; historic houses; boats; museums and galleries; and sports clubs.

Finding a venue Popular venues get booked up months or even years ahead, particularly over the summer, so it's never too early to look. Word of mouth is a good start, or look in the Yellow Pages, local papers, hotel guides, wedding magazines and on the internet. Your local register office has a list of licensed venues countrywide. There are even venue-finding companies.

When you've found a venue, the first questions to ask are: Is it available and is it the right size? Is it close to the church? Find out if there's an in-house wedding coordinator; whether there will be other weddings there that day; whether or not there's an in-house caterer; whether they can recommend other services, such as musicians; and how late the reception can carry on. In the case of a hotel, ask if they'll offer special rates for guests staying the night. Is there enough room for dancing? Is there ample parking? Do the staff seem efficient and helpful? Ask how the venue's charges work, what types of reception you could have and, finally, for a written estimate. If you're happy, reserve the day and find out how much deposit is required. Ask for details of your booking in writing.

Above **If you want to get married in your local church, your first step is to make an appointment with your minister, who will discuss procedures and fees with you and may ask you to attend prenuptial counselling.**

Right **If you have access to a big garden or a friendly farmer's field, a marquee will allow you to entertain a large number of guests. Get several quotes and think carefully about any extras you may need, such as flooring, lighting, heating and furniture.**

Religious ceremonies

The Church of England The basic arrangements for the Churches of England and Wales are similar. Couples can marry on any day of the week, though Saturday is the most popular day, between 8am and 6pm. Arrange a meeting with your minister, who may also want you to attend some prenuptial counselling. He or she will require various personal details and will talk to you about church fees, calling the banns and forms of service.

Banns are called on three Sundays before the wedding, which then has to take place within three months. If you live in different parishes, banns are called in both. To be married in a parish, you need to be resident there or be a regular worshipper. Alternatively, you can be married by common licence, which requires you to be resident for only 15 days before the licence is granted and does away with the need for banns. This is also valid for three months. In unusual situations, such as when couples wish to marry outside their normal parishes, a special licence can be applied for from the Archbishop of Canterbury; talk to your minister about this first. Ask whether your minister allows photography or videography during the service, or the throwing of confetti.

The rehearsal It's usual to hold a wedding rehearsal near the day, so you and your fiancé can get a feel for the ceremony and iron out any problems. The couple, the best man, the attendants and the couple's families usually attend, and the event is an opportunity to have a meal or get-together afterwards.

The service The bride walks down the aisle on her father's right arm, followed by her attendants. The bridegroom and best man will be waiting at the top of the aisle to take their places on the bride's

If you're hiring a marquee, think about the number of guests. Will there be a sit-down meal or dancing? Will you need buffet or bar areas? Think about flooring, lighting, heating, furniture and decorations. You may need service tents for catering staff and loos for guests. Make sure there's sufficient parking and remember that lighting and heating costs are higher for an evening than a daytime reception, and for a winter rather than a summer wedding. Spare a thought for your neighbours if you have a reception at home. Warn them in advance and tell them when the music will stop. Ask your marquee company if it can use a 'sound ceiling' to limit noise.

right. The bride hands her bouquet to her chief bridesmaid (or mother). The minister welcomes everyone, then there may be a hymn, followed by readings (normally two), another hymn or psalm, an address by the minister, and the marriage itself.

The bride's father takes his daughter's right hand and gives it to the minister, who passes it to the groom. The couple take their vows and the best man gives the ring(s) to the groom, or the minister receives them on an open prayer book. The bride's father and the best man return to their seats. The newlyweds follow the minister to the altar for prayers. A hymn may be sung before the final blessing. The minister is followed by the bride and groom, their parents, the best man and the chief bridesmaid into the vestry to sign the register. Afterwards, the bride and groom (with the bride on the groom's left), followed by the attendants, the chief bridesmaid and best man, the bride's mother and groom's father, and the groom's mother and bride's father, process down the aisle.

Second marriages

The general rule in the Church of England is that divorcees cannot have a full marriage service (though there is scope for ministers to make personal decisions in this matter). A Service of Blessing is the alternative, which must be preceded by a civil ceremony since it is not a marriage service. The form of the service is at the discretion of the minister, so discuss with him or her the question of music, readings and whether the bride is given away. Denominations such as the Methodists, United Reformed Church and the Church of Scotland may be more willing to marry divorced persons. In the Roman Catholic Church, second marriages can take place in church only if the previous marriage has been annulled or the spouse has died.

Opposite **One of the benefits offered by nearly all licensed venues is that of being able to hold a reception as well as a wedding ceremony there. An increasing number of venues also employ in-house wedding coordinators to help couples make their arrangements. Your local register office or the General Register Office for England and Wales can provide lists of venues. Here, the scene is set for a low-key and intimate reception for immediate family and close friends.**

Above **A magnificent array of flowers in an old village church, bringing all the beauty of a summer garden indoors. Some churches have resident flower clubs, whose members may be willing to produce arrangements for weddings. Your minister will be able to give you details.**

The Church of Scotland Religious ceremonies can be conducted anywhere (inside or out, in a church or a non-religious building) by a minister (though this is at his or her discretion). There are no residency requirements for couples, though they must give notice at the register office in the district in which they're marrying 15 days before the ceremony.

The Roman Catholic Church Roman Catholic priests don't act on behalf of the state as Anglican ministers do, so couples marrying in Catholic churches must obtain a certificate to marry from their local register office. After the service, the wedding is registered for the civil authorities by someone specially authorized to do so, often the priest himself or a parishioner.

Mixed-faith marriages Catholics marrying non-Catholics, whether they marry in a Catholic church or not, must obtain a dispensation from their parish priest. It may be possible to get married in one church and have a blessing in the other, or to have ministers of both religions present at the service.

Above left and right **Pew-ends are a delightful way to decorate a church aisle. Here, loops of twisted ivy have been placed over the pew-ends. Roses add scent and colour.**

Readings It's usual to have at least one Bible reading, but you could have a non-religious reading (see opposite). Some ideas are given below.
- ♥ 1 Corinthians 13 '…The greatest of these is love'
- ♥ Colossians 3:12–17 'You are the people of God'
- ♥ 1 John (Epistle) 4:7–12 'God is love'

Other religions Church of England ministers act on behalf of the state. Ministers of other religions do not, so there are civil requirements to be fulfilled as well as the religious service. Couples must obtain a licence or certificate to marry from their local register office. Jewish synagogues employ a marriage secretary to check that civil requirements are met and to register weddings. Churches of other denominations, mosques and temples may also have a person who has been authorized by the state to fulfil this function. If there is no such person, couples can have a civil ceremony in a register office before their religious service.

Civil weddings

Register office ceremonies

You can get married in any register office in England and Wales. However, you must both visit your local register office first to 'give notice' of your intention to marry. If you and your fiancé live in different areas, visit each office (you must have been resident for seven days before giving notice). Giving notice involves providing personal details and signing a declaration that there is no legal impediment to the marriage. After 16 days, the marriage can take place (the certificate issued after giving notice is valid for one year, so the wedding must take place within this period). Register offices are open during office hours from Monday to Friday, and on Saturday mornings, although these are often heavily booked. Check how many guests the office seats. The ceremony takes around 20 minutes and two people are required to be witnesses.

Ceremonies in licensed venues

Over 2,000 venues in England and Wales have been licensed by their local authority to hold civil wedding ceremonies. These include hotels, stately homes, restaurants and more unusual places such as football clubs, cinemas, boats and zoos. To obtain a licence, venues must be permanent, fixed structures, open to the public and unconnected with religion. Your local register office or the General Register Office for England and Wales can supply a list of premises. Check whether the venues you're interested in have facilities for receptions as well as ceremonies. Bigger venues often have wedding coordinators to help organize the day. Couples getting married in a licensed venue should contact the registrar there as well as in their own area, to check that they are able to officiate and to run through details such as music and readings.

Fees

Whether you marry in a register office or a licensed venue, fees are charged for the notice of marriage, for the registrar's services and for a copy of the marriage certificate. Contact your local register office to check current charges. These are the basics, but if you're marrying in a licensed venue there will, of course, be other costs involved.

Scotland, Northern Ireland and Ireland

In Scotland, Northern Ireland and Ireland, a civil ceremony must be held in a register office. In Scotland there are no residency requirements, so couples give notice at the register office in which they are to marry, not their local office. In Northern Ireland, one partner must be resident for at least seven days in the area in which the couple wish to marry. In Ireland, one partner must be resident for at least seven days.

Music and readings

Music and readings at civil weddings must be non-religious. For ideas about music, see page 92. You could have a couple of readings during the ceremony, taken from your favourite poems, novels or songs. Ask the registrar to approve your choices before the day. A few suggestions are given below.

♥ Shakespeare, sonnet xviii, 'Let me not to the marriage of true minds / Admit impediments'

♥ Kahlil Gibran, *The Prophet*

♥ Christopher Marlowe, *The Passionate Shepherd to His Love*, 'Come live with me and be my love'

♥ Sir Philip Sidney, *The Bargain*, 'My true love hath my heart, and I have his'

♥ Ben Jonson, *To Celia*, 'Drink to me only with thine eyes'

Alternative ceremonies

Alternative wedding ceremonies such as handfastings are not legally recognized, so you'll have to have a civil ceremony as well in order to be legally married.

Flowers A wedding somehow isn't a wedding without flowers. They add beauty, colour and scent as nothing else can, bringing the outdoors indoors on even the dullest days of the year.

Finding the right florist Ask friends for recommendations. Your caterer or reception venue may also have some ideas. Otherwise, make appointments with several local florists. Ask if they have a portfolio, so you can see whether you like their work. Look for someone who is helpful, sympathetic to your requests and easy to get on with. If possible, take along fabric swatches or pictures of your dress and your attendants' outfits, since they're the natural starting point for choosing a colour scheme. If you've been inspired by books or magazines, take these along, particularly if you don't know the names of the flowers you like. Look at flowers in the shop and don't be afraid to ask what they are if you're unsure. Other things can be used in decorations, too, such as ribbon, fruits and vegetables, seed heads and dried flowers. Branches of twisted willow hung with fairy lights look magical and could be sprayed white or silver for a wintry feel. Hops create a rustic, autumnal atmosphere, and if yours is a Christmas wedding, why not go to town with Christmas trees and baubles?

Tell your florist what your budget is. Remember that the more complicated and time-consuming the arrangement (such as wired bouquets, floral 'trees', garlands or floral arches), the more expensive it is. Discuss what props you might want (vases, candelabra, pedestals) and ask who will do the arranging on the day. If the florist is unfamiliar with the venues you're using, ask if they will visit them to help you both decide what sort of arrangements you need. Failing that, show them photographs. Once you've decided what you want, get a written estimate. Find out when the flowers will be delivered and give someone the task of being there to receive them. Ask for bouquets to be labelled, so there isn't any confusion about which is which.

Flower checklist

☐ bride's bouquet

☐ bouquets or posies for the bridesmaids

☐ corsages for the mothers

☐ buttonholes for the groom, best man, ushers and fathers

☐ arrangements for the church or civil venue

☐ arrangements for the reception

Saving money Although many flowers are available all year, those that are in season are usually the best value. Look at your venues and see where arrangements will have most impact. One or two beautiful arrangements placed strategically are a better bet than lots of small ones dotted around. You may be able to make your flowers do double duty by transporting the easily movable ones from your ceremony venue to your reception. Give someone (perhaps a couple of ushers) the task of doing this straight after the ceremony. If you're getting married in church and yours isn't the only wedding that day, you may be able to share your flowers with the other couple, therefore dividing the cost. Ask for help from friends or relatives who are good flower arrangers and ask if they'll provide flowers from their own gardens. Displays don't have to be sophisticated to look good – cottage-garden flowers simply arranged have a charm of their own. Another idea is to plant up pots with bedding plants or bulbs in time for them to be in bloom at your wedding. Spring bulbs would work well.

Colour ideas

White or cream The classic wedding colours, they look stunning against a background of rich green foliage.

Pastels Pretty, soft and romantic. Use a mixture, single shades or in combination with white or cream.

Deep shades Dramatic and sophisticated as a contrast to a pale wedding dress. Handle with care so that they don't overwhelm.

Brights For a tropical touch. Best suited to the brilliant light of summer. Again, handle with care.

Flowers for all seasons

Spring Anemones, bluebells, camellias, crocuses, forget-me-nots, grape hyacinths, hellebores, hyacinths, lilies of the valley, narcissi, pansies, ranunculuses, tulips, violets.

Summer Campanulas, cornflowers, delphiniums, hydrangeas, gypsophila, jasmine, lady's mantle, larkspurs, marguerites, peonies, phlox, roses, scabious, stocks, sweet peas.

Autumn Amaranthus, chrysanthemums, cosmos, dahlias, hydrangeas, Japanese anemones, Michaelmas daisies, scabious.

Winter Heather, hellebores, irises, primulas, snowdrops, winter jasmine.

All year Alstroemeria, carnations, chrysanthemums, freesias, gerberas, gypsophila, lilies, orchids, roses.

Opposite top **Cream garden roses make a simple but romantic posy for a bride or bridesmaid.**

Opposite centre **Decorated chair backs look striking and aren't hard to create. If you can't decorate every chair, reserve this treatment for the high table or your and your fiancé's chairs. Here, a head of soft blue hydrangea is tied with sky-blue ribbon.**

Opposite below **An enamel pail decorated with blue gingham ribbon and filled with headily scented paperwhite narcissi makes a charmingly rustic flower arrangement.**

Below **It's important for your bouquet to complement the style of your dress. Here, a simple, slim-cut silk dress demands a modern and minimalist bouquet: three exquisite white arum lilies loosely tied with white ribbon.**

The bride's bouquet A beautiful bouquet or posy is the quintessential bridal accessory. The classic bridal bouquet is a 'shower', a teardrop-shaped, wired arrangement of flowers and foliage. Recently, it's become popular to have a bouquet or posy where the flowers are arranged into a bunch and the stems are tied. (Incidentally, a posy is simply a smaller arrangement than a bouquet.) A tightly packed bouquet, arranged into a dome shape, can look very stylish, particularly if it's composed of a single type of flower, such as roses or tulips. You could have a domed bouquet where the colour is graduated across it, going from cream to pale, then deeper pink. Tied bouquets look attractive with pretty ribbon wrapped round the stems and tied into a bow. A sheaf of 'architectural' flowers, such as moth orchids or arum lilies, gives a sophisticated, modern look. When you're choosing your bouquet, take your dress as your starting point. Your flowers should match it in scale and style. For instance, with a sleek, slim-cut dress, a sheaf of flowers or a long shower would work well, while a full-skirted, grand gown is the perfect partner for a generous bouquet. Although flowers are the stars of a bouquet, foliage plays a key role in offsetting them, so ask your florist what they'll be using. Bouquets can also incorporate dried seed heads, rosehips, catkins, berries, fruits (such as Cape gooseberries, chillies or crabapples) or shells. For a wildly romantic look, cover your bouquet in fine tulle or net.

Preserving your bouquet Even if you throw your bouquet at the end of your reception, you may want to ask someone to retrieve it so you can preserve the flowers permanently. If you've pressed flowers before or dried them in silica gel (from craft shops), you may want to have a go yourself. Otherwise, there are companies which specialize in pressing or preserving flowers under glass.

Flowers for scent Using flowers which smell as good as they look adds another sensory dimension to bouquets. Some of the most sweetly scented are roses, freesias, gardenias, jasmine, lilies, lilies of the valley, peonies, pinks, sweet peas, stephanotis and tuberoses. You could also try herbs, such as lavender, rosemary, thyme or lemon balm.

The language of flowers Originally, bridal bouquets consisted of herbs, whose perfumes were thought to ward off evil spirits. There are meanings to many flowers; below are a few wedding favourites.

Alstroemeria: Friendship	**Ivy:** Wedded love
Carnation: The bonds of love	**Lavender:** Devotion
Chrysanthemum: Joy, long life, truth	**Lily:** Majesty
Freesia: Innocence	**Rose:** Love
Gypsophila: Fruitful marriage	**Violet:** Faithfulness

Opposite **Seed heads, berries and even fruits can be used alongside flowers in bouquets. Here, plump poppy seed heads contrast with the softer forms of such flowers as roses and hydrangeas.**

Above **In this tightly packed posy of cream and white roses, red hypericum berries add a dash of rich colour.**

Below **Flowers can be used to capture the essence of the seasons. Here, the slender, airy lines of white longiflorum lilies and loosestrife create a light, summery look.**

Flowers for the bridal party

Bridesmaids Bridesmaids' flowers should complement those of the bride, although they don't have to be exactly the same. Small bouquets or posies, tied or wired, are the obvious choice, particularly for adult bridesmaids. For young bridesmaids, little baskets, filled with flowers or confetti, are easy to carry, as are floral circlets, decorated hoops and floral balls (flowers are stuck all over a ball of florist's foam and a ribbon is attached to make a handle). A single, large bloom (such as a peony or gardenia) looks striking with ribbon tied around its stem immediately below the flower head. Alternatively, bridesmaids needn't carry flowers at all: little bags (which could be filled with confetti), lucky horseshoes, fairy wands, dolls or teddies (which your pageboys might like, too) make nice presents for young attendants to keep afterwards.

Buttonholes Buttonholes are normally worn by the bridegroom, best man, ushers and fathers of the couple, and consist of a single bloom or sprig of flowers with a little bit of foliage. Roses or carnations are popular buttonhole choices, while for gorgeous scent you could try lily of the valley, jasmine or stephanotis. A single, bold flower such as a camellia or orchid looks modern. Make sure buttonholes are securely fastened, and don't forget to give someone extra pins in case there aren't enough to go round.

Corsages These may be worn by the mothers and grandmothers of the couple and are the same size or a little larger than a buttonhole. Corsages are pinned onto the outfit, usually on the chest, collar, lapel or wrist. Bear in mind that, with clothes that are made of very fine fabric, the corsage should be small and light so it doesn't drag or tear.

Opposite top **If your young bridesmaids are to carry bouquets or posies, make sure that they are an appropriate size and are easy to carry. This posy's stem is just right for small hands. Other ideas include hoops and flower- or confetti-filled baskets.**

Opposite below **Roses are the classic wedding flower and make elegant, fragrant buttonholes. Here, partnering them with hydrangea flowers gives an old favourite a new twist.**

Above **Give your best man or chief usher extra pins to secure buttonholes, which are usually worn by the bridegroom, best man, ushers and fathers of the bride and groom.**

Below **Though not for carrying around all day, a garland of ivy formed into a romantic swag between two bouquets guarantees that these young bridesmaids will make a dramatic entrance at the wedding ceremony.**

Flowers for the ceremony

Church weddings Check with your minister if there's anywhere he or she doesn't want you to put an arrangement. Areas to think about include the entrance, porch or gateway; pew-ends; windowsills; the bottom and top of the aisle (perhaps a floral arch or pedestal arrangement); the font; pillars; the pulpit; and the altar.

Civil weddings Because of the number of ceremonies that take place in register offices, it's not feasible to decorate them for each couple. You'll have to add colour and decoration with your bouquets and buttonholes. If you're holding your civil ceremony in a licensed venue, you should be able to have as many floral decorations as you want. Many venues have wedding coordinators, who may be able to recommend a florist.

Confetti The Romans used to shower newlyweds with almonds, a symbol of fertility. Rice later came into vogue, and now confetti is usually made of paper. Check with your wedding venue that they're happy for your guests to throw confetti. Some aren't, so if necessary insert a slip of paper into your orders of service asking people to refrain. Some couples like to provide guests with confetti, leaving it loose in baskets, bags or little cones of coloured paper for them to collect after the ceremony. Paper confetti is now available in myriad shapes, colours and sizes, but there are alternatives. Try dried or fresh flower petals (roses are the obvious choice) from a florist, obliging friends with well-stocked gardens or a specialist company; or bottles of soap bubbles for guests to blow over you. A word of warning about paper confetti: it can stain fabric badly if it gets wet, so take extra care with your dress if the heavens open.

Many churches aren't keen on paper confetti because of the mess it leaves, but there are biodegradable alternatives.

Opposite above **Birdseed** is one confetti alternative, here placed in little greaseproof-paper bags secured with raffia.

Opposite below **Rose** petals are another choice and can be used fresh or dried. Leave in baskets, paper cones or little boxes for your guests to collect after the ceremony.

Right Strategically placing flower arrangements to emphasize focal points such as windows, alcoves and doorways can make a few displays go a long way.

Flowers for the reception Areas to think about include the entrance; large expanses of wall which need 'breaking up'; and features which lend themselves to decoration, such as alcoves. In a marquee, you could think about decorating the entrance and poles with garlands, and having hanging arrangements. Strings of fairy or carnival lights look magical at night (though if you intend to use them outdoors, make sure they're designed for this) and it's possible to hire black marquee linings dotted with fairy lights to create a starry-sky effect. Candles, from church candles to nightlights, create a romantic atmosphere, though remember that any naked flame poses a fire risk. The top table is normally decorated, perhaps with an edging or garland of flowers, and you'll undoubtedly want table decorations (see page 106) and something for the table with the cake.

♥ It seems a shame that wedding flowers are only needed for a day, so encourage friends and family to take away portable arrangements at the end of the day so they can carry on enjoying them at home.

Seasonal flower and decoration ideas

Spring Eggs (blown-out or hard-boiled) coloured with food dye or tied round with ribbon; tulips, hyacinths, pansies, primroses, bluebells and daffodils; apple or cherry blossom; peonies.

Summer Old-fashioned roses, sweet peas, larkspur, stocks, gypsophila and lady's mantle; soft fruits or grapes; herbs; seashells.

Autumn Seed heads and nuts sprayed gold; chrysanthemums and Michaelmas daisies; pumpkins, blackberries and apples; hops; rosehips; moss; ears of wheat or corn.

Winter Cinnamon sticks; ivy, holly and mistletoe; pine cones; red apples; church candles; red roses; nuts; crackers; Christmas baubles; twisted willow sprayed white or silver.

Opposite Tied bunches of herbs such as rosemary, thyme or lavender at each place setting will appeal to guests' senses of sight and smell.

Right above A distinctive china bowl is filled to the brim with cream roses to make a luxurious centrepiece. All sorts of containers can be used for flower arrangements, even jam jars, which look charming filled with posies of cottage-garden flowers.

Right centre Candles always create a magical atmosphere. Here, chunky church candles are partnered with single orchid blooms placed in glass dessert bowls filled with water.

Right below Painting inexpensive terracotta flowerpots white and filling them with seasonal flowers – here, narcissi and hyacinths – is a simple but effective idea.

Music You don't have to be a musician to know that music creates a special atmosphere at a wedding. Remember that, while music for a church wedding can be religious or secular, the pieces you choose for a civil ceremony must be non-religious.

Church weddings Your minister may know the organist's repertoire, or talk to the organist. There may also be a choir, which is useful for giving a good lead in the hymns. Many church organists are amateurs, so go with what they feel happy playing. Be realistic: if you've heard a piece on a CD played by a full orchestra, it won't sound the same played on a small, village organ. You could have other musicians at your service, such as a string quartet, harpist, professional choir or solo singer. It's courteous to ask the organist first and to check your choice of music with the minister.

The service The musical formats for Church of England and Roman Catholic weddings are similar, though the latter may incorporate a nuptial mass, which can be sung. The organist usually plays as guests arrive, then for the entrance of the bride. There are two or three hymns (before or between readings, before the prayers and before the final blessing), and/or a psalm. There is usually music during the signing of the register, then a triumphal piece announces the exit of the bride and groom.

Money Your minister will give you the rates for the organist and choir, which vary from church to church. Prices for amateur musicians are lower than for professionals, who may require travel expenses as well. Expect any musician to increase their fee by between 50 and 100 per cent if the service is being recorded or videoed. Tell your church, organist and musicians in advance if you want to video or record the wedding. Fees should be settled before the service by the best man on behalf of the groom.

Civil weddings You may want to have music before your ceremony, for the entrance of the bride, for the signing of the register and the exit of the bride and groom. If you're getting married in a register office, space will be limited, so a small ensemble of musicians or recorded music are the best options. Licensed venues offer more scope for bigger groups. Wherever you're getting married, the registrar must approve your choice of music.

The reception Having music at a reception helps to create a relaxed and welcoming atmosphere. You may want background music as guests arrive, or a band to play for a dance. A DJ is an alternative to live music. Decide which styles of music you feel comfortable with. Consider, too, your venue's acoustics and the number of guests you're inviting and therefore the noise they'll make. Your guests should be able to hear the music but still make conversation. If you're having a dance and want to be able to impress your guests when you take to the floor for the first time, take a few dance lessons.

First dance ideas

I Will Always Love You (Whitney Houston)

You're My Everything (Barry White)

Love is a Many Splendored Thing (Nat King Cole)

My Heart Will Go On (Celine Dion)

Love is All Around (Wet Wet Wet)

We Have All the Time in the World
  (Louis Armstrong)

Booking musicians Prompt return of calls and good presentation of publicity material indicate professionalism. Ask for a demonstration tape, and if possible go to a live performance. Make sure you get details of arrival time, playing time, finishing time and fee confirmed in writing. Check whether the fee includes travel expenses, and whether you're expected to feed your musicians. Give your musicians clear directions to your wedding and make sure they can park and unload equipment easily. If you know what sort of music you want, you can look for specialist groups; otherwise, music agencies deal with lots of different groups and can help you decide what to choose. Your reception venue may specify a time, often around midnight, at which music has to stop.

Suggested music for the ceremony

✠ indicates works which are sacred and therefore not suitable for civil weddings

The entrance of the bride

Arrival of the Queen of Sheba, Handel

Here Comes the Bride from *Lohengrin*, Wagner

Grand March from *Aida*, Verdi

Hornpipe from *Water Music*, Handel

✠ *Prelude* from *Te Deum*, Charpentier

Trumpet Tune, Purcell

Trumpet Voluntary, Clarke

Wedding March from *The Marriage of Figaro*, Mozart

♥ A hymn would also be suitable.

The signing of the register

Adagio, Albinoni

Air on a G String, Bach

Air from *Water Music*, Handel

Canon, Pachelbel

✠ *Jesu, Joy of Man's Desiring*, Bach

✠ *Sheep May Safely Graze*, Bach

Choir pieces for the signing of the register

✠ *Ave Verum Corpus*, Mozart

✠ *God Be in My Head*, Walford Davies

✠ *Jesu, Joy of Man's Desiring*, Bach

✠ *The Lord Bless You and Keep You*, Rutter

Solo voice pieces for the signing of the register

✠ *Ave Maria*, Bach/Gounod

✠ *Ave Maria*, Schubert

✠ *Panis Angelicus*, Franck

Exit of the bride and groom

Crown Imperial, Walton

Final from *Symphony No 1*, Vierne

Prelude and Fugue in B, Dupré

Toccata, Widor

Wedding March, Mendelssohn

♥ The Charpentier, Purcell and Clarke pieces for the entrance of the bride would also be suitable.

Psalms

✠ Psalm 23:'The Lord is My Shepherd'

✠ Psalm 67:'God Be Merciful Unto Us and Bless Us'

✠ Psalm 121:'I Will Lift up Mine Eyes'

✠ Psalm 150:'O Praise God in His Holiness'

Hymns

✠ *Come Down O Love Divine*

✠ *Glorious Things of Thee Are Spoken*

✠ *Love Divine All Loves Excelling*

✠ *O Praise Ye the Lord*

✠ *Praise My Soul the King of Heaven*

✠ *The Lord's My Shepherd*

Photography and videography A wedding day is over all too quickly. Photographs and videos will allow you to revisit yours whenever you want. Good professionals do the job comprehensively, artistically and efficiently, but don't forget that pictures and videos taken by friends have a charm and intimacy of their own.

Finding the right photographer and videographer The same sorts of questions that you apply to your search for a photographer apply to a videographer. Personal recommendation is a good start. Otherwise, see several photographers to compare styles, service and prices. Find out whether they are members of professional associations (see opposite), have won any awards or are affiliated to photography companies such as Kodak. Ask to see a number of weddings they have photographed – as many pictures as possible, not just a few of their best. You're after someone with whom you get on, who is sympathetic to your needs, whose work you like and who deals with you efficiently and professionally. They also need to be able to work without getting in everyone's way or holding things up. Make sure that the photographer you see will actually attend your wedding, and check that they have professional indemnity insurance in case things go wrong.

Tell your photographer exactly what sort of pictures you want. If you want group shots, give them a list, with copies to the ushers so they can marshal your guests. Decide if you want to have photographs taken before the wedding while you get ready. If you're marrying in church, ask your minister whether pictures can be taken of the ceremony. Plan a realistic schedule that won't keep guests hanging around, a common complaint against wedding photographers. Have a back-up plan in case it rains. Ideally, your photographer should visit your ceremony and reception venues so that they can find the best places to take pictures. Decide whether you'd like your photographer to stay for the whole reception or just part of it.

Remember that the photographer owns the copyright of your pictures and will retain the negatives. Check whether your deal includes all the photographs taken or just a selection, and whether you get a presentation album. Ask how much reprints cost. The cost of a photographer varies enormously. The best may charge thousands and, while there are excellent photographers who cost a great deal less, think twice if someone is suspiciously cheap.

Styles Many photographers now favour a candid, 'reportage' style in which the subjects are relaxed rather than posed, feeling that they best capture the spirit of the day. Others favour traditional, posed group shots, which many brides like

Above right **Having a video made can add an extra dimension to your memories of your wedding, allowing you to relive key moments of the day such as the ceremony, speeches and first dance.**

Right **With photographers, as with videographers, it's essential to do your homework before you make a booking or hand over any money. Personal recommendation is always the best way to start, but membership of professional bodies and prizes won are other indications to look out for. Ask plenty of questions, take your time when looking at someone's work, and make sure you're clear about what the price does and doesn't include.**

as a family record. Don't be pushed into having anything you don't want and remember that you should be able to have a mixture of shots. All sorts of styles and effects are possible: black and white; colour; sepia or hand-coloured; digitally manipulated with computers; cross-processed, which gives intense colour effects; and soft focus.

Professional associations

British Institute of Professional Photography (BIPP):
LBIPP = Licentiate; ABIPP = Associate; FBIPP = Fellow

Master Photographers' Association (MPA):
LMPA = Licentiate; AMPA = Associate; FMPA = Fellow

Royal Photographic Society (RPS):
LRPS = Licentiate; ARPS = Associate; FRPS = Fellow

Irish Professional Photographers' Association (IPPA)

The Society of Wedding and Portrait Photographers

Above **A smartly uniformed chauffeur at the wheel of a wedding car adds to the sense of occasion.**

Above right **Vintage cars are always popular for weddings and are great fun. There are lots of other possibilities, however, from romantic horse-drawn carriages to hot-air balloons. It's worth visiting any companies you're interested in to check how well maintained their vehicles are.**

Transport Travelling to and from your wedding in a splendid old Daimler or romantic horse-drawn carriage is far from essential, but it's one of the things that makes the day fun and special. If hiring something is out of the question financially, ask among your friends to see if there's a vintage-car enthusiast among them or someone who owns a smart sports car. Any car can be smartened up with a good wash and polish and the addition of ribbon or flowers.

The groom and best man normally travel to the ceremony under their own steam, while the bride is treated to something special which can then take the newlyweds to their reception. They also need to be taken from the reception to their first-night hotel, though probably not in the same vehicle, which will otherwise have to wait until the reception ends. The bridesmaids and mother of the bride are usually taken to the ceremony together, before the bride and her father.

Types of transport There's nothing as romantic as a horse-drawn coach or carriage. Cinderella-style coaches, landaus and so on can be hired, complete with liveried coachmen. Vintage cars have an air of old-fashioned luxury, though modern limousines, white and black taxis, and sports cars are also popular. If you're after something unconventional, what about a classic Harley-Davidson (though it's impractical if your dress is long and full)? If you can ride, try local riding schools and equestrian centres for four-legged transport. If you're having a riverside reception, rowing off into the sunset will give your guests something to talk about (you can arrange for a car to pick you up downstream and take you to your hotel). However, perhaps the ultimate in grand exits is to go up, up and away in a helicopter or a hot-air balloon.

Transport tips

♥ Before you book your transport, think about practicalities such as the time of year and weather – important considerations if you want an open carriage – and your dress, which may take up a fair bit of room. If your dress is full with a long train, it could crease if you choose a car which hasn't got enough room in the back.

♥ Book as far ahead of your wedding as possible to be sure of getting what you want.

♥ Go to see companies so you can check that their vehicles are well maintained.

♥ Get a written estimate and check whether charges are by the hour or are at a set rate, and how much mileage is included. Ask whether your transport will be decorated for the day and if chauffeurs or coachmen will be in uniform.

♥ If you're booking an old car, ask what happens if it breaks down.

♥ Take traffic into account when you're working out your timetable and check the week before the wedding whether there are any roadworks on your route.

♥ Companies may be able to provide champagne in your vehicle after the ceremony.

♥ Confirm your booking a week or so before the day, and make sure that your honeymoon luggage is sent ahead to your hotel or loaded into your car.

Above **Before you book your transport, take into account the time of year you're getting married – an open carriage is wonderful on a sunny summer's day but not much fun if it's cold. Think about how full your dress is and whether it will fit comfortably into the car.**

Below **Most hire companies will decorate vehicles for weddings. If you have something specific in mind, discuss this when you make your booking. Some companies also provide champagne for couples to sip on their way from the ceremony to the reception.**

The reception timetable

♥ Couples often have photographs taken after the wedding ceremony but it's important not to keep guests waiting for ages before the reception.

♥ The bride and groom arrive first, then the bridesmaids, best man and parents.

♥ A receiving line lets you welcome your guests and gives them the chance to congratulate you. The usual order is: bride's mother and father, groom's mother and father, bride, groom, chief bridesmaid and best man. If step-parents are involved, it's up to you whether to include them. If you don't want a formal receiving line, you and your families, or just you and your groom, could stand in a group to welcome people. With lots of guests, a receiving line can be lengthy, so you could simply mingle.

♥ The meal. If the minister who married you is at the reception, ask him or her to say grace.

♥ The speeches and toasts (see below).

♥ The cutting of the cake (see page 113).

♥ Receptions often go on into the evening with a dance and even another meal, carrying on after the speeches and cake, or after a short break. Don't keep guests hanging around with nowhere to go.

♥ The departure of the bride and groom. The tradition is that guests stay to see newlyweds off. Consider this when you're planning when to go.

The speeches There can be few grooms, fathers or best men who look forward to giving their speech. However, speeches are an important opportunity to voice the thoughts and emotions which the day gives rise to, and wedding guests make a receptive audience. The normal order of speeches is: the bride's father (or whoever gave her away); the groom; then the best man. Sometimes the bride and/or chief bridesmaid will speak. They can be slotted in wherever seems appropriate, but make sure the toasts are still made and answered.

♥ Keep to the point – five to 10 minutes at most.

♥ Smile and look round at your guests. If you look happy and confident, you'll probably sound it, too.

♥ If you're not naturally witty, don't try too hard. Be sincere and speak from the heart.

♥ Prepare well in advance – not the night before.

♥ Practise your speech out loud a few times and time it to make sure it doesn't overrun. If possible, read it to someone whose opinion you trust.

♥ If you're an inexperienced speaker, write the speech out in full rather than in note form.

♥ Be funny if you can, but avoid anything smutty or embarrassing. Elderly relatives will be listening as well as your friends, so it must be suitable for all.

♥ Keep your sentences short and your language conversational and informal.

♥ If you're not used to speaking in public, use a microphone if there is one. If not, lift your head and project your voice – don't talk into your notes. You'll need to speak up to be heard at the back of a room.

♥ Don't rush or you'll fall over your words. Take a deep breath and take your time.

The bride's father His speech focuses on his daughter. He should say:

♥ how pleased he is to see so many family members and friends at the wedding;

♥ how proud he is of his daughter (he may want to recount some stories from her childhood);

♥ how pleased he is to welcome his new son-in-law into the family.

He finishes with a toast to 'the bride and groom'.

The groom He answers the bride's father, thanking him for the toast (he usually gets in a mention here of his 'wife', which is guaranteed to prompt applause from the guests!). His main duty is thanking people:

- everyone who's come to the wedding;
- everyone who's helped to organize the wedding and reception, such as both sets of parents (and anyone else who's contributed financially or otherwise);
- his parents for all their help and support over the years (here, he may give a gift or bouquet to his and the bride's mother);
- his best man;
- his wife for marrying him and being such a beautiful bride;
- the attendants for doing such a good job.

He finishes by toasting 'absent friends', then 'the bridesmaids' (and/or pageboys).

The best man He has a challenge, as he is expected to be funny. He should:

- thank the groom for his words and his toast to the attendants;
- read out messages or cards from absent friends;
- recount some amusing anecdotes about the groom;
- talk about the bride and say what a good couple she and the groom make.

He finishes by toasting 'Mr and Mrs…' and announcing the cutting of the cake.

Above **Placing a favour at each place setting makes everyone feel welcome and is a good icebreaker.**

Below **A reception awaits its guests. Seating plans take time to draw up but prevent a scramble for places and help to place people together who you feel will get on well.**

Left and opposite below **Canapés are a popular way to feed wedding guests, but if people are expected to stand to eat them, the reception should be kept fairly short. If they're taking the place of a meal, make sure that there are plenty of them and that waiting staff circulate them efficiently.**

Below **A sit-down meal is one of the most expensive catering options, but gives everyone the chance to take the** weight off their feet and socialize over their food and wine. A meal like this could be a three-course plated affair or a buffet from which guests help themselves.

Opposite above **Remember that the number of waiting staff you hire will have a considerable impact on the overall cost of your reception. You should also check if and when you will have to start paying them overtime.**

Food and drink Weddings involve guests in expense and travel, so your side of the bargain is to provide them with a reception at which there is ample to eat and drink. The golden rule is therefore obvious: don't invite more guests than you can afford to entertain properly. You'll need to know the number of guests before you can get quotes from venues or caterers, so make this a priority.

Types of reception

♥ A sit-down, three-course meal is the traditional 'wedding breakfast' and is the most formal and expensive option. A cold meal is fine for summer; a hot one is more welcoming in winter. You could have a mainly cold meal with one hot element such as potatoes.

♥ A buffet gives guests lots of choice and should be cheaper than a sit-down meal because there are fewer staff. You could have guests seated at tables or standing, though this is less comfortable for everyone. Even if most people stand, there must be enough seats for the elderly, pregnant women and so on. Any reception where guests are expected to stand should be kept fairly short.

♥ Canapés have come a long way since the days of soggy vol-au-vents. If they're taking the place of a meal, they must be substantial enough, there must be plenty of them and waiting staff must do a good job of circulating.

♥ A barbecue could be fun, but is vulnerable to bad weather. Another idea is to have food stations or stalls around a marquee serving different things.

♥ A cost-effective option is to have a tea-time reception at which you offer little sandwiches, scones, cakes and biscuits. It would be relatively easy to do home catering for this type of reception.

♥ Choose ingredients which are in season, as they should be tastier and better value.

♥ There's a trend for having traditional, hearty fare such as bangers and mash, shepherd's pie or fish and chips. This can be good value and fun but needs to done with a bit of style so it doesn't look ordinary.

Choosing a caterer Start with personal recommendations. Otherwise, obtain several quotes and ask to see sample menus. It should be possible to mix and match between set menus if you don't like everything on them. Ask for edible samples, too. Get a written quote and find out when your caterer needs to know final numbers. They'll need to be told if there any vegetarians or guests with other dietary requirements. You could include a slip of paper with your invitations asking people to let you know.

Think very carefully before you or any of your family undertake to cater for the reception. However good a home cook someone is, mass catering is a different matter. It's a lot of work and will need to be planned like a military operation. You'll also need plenty of volunteers to help. However, if you can do it, it will save you a lot of money.

Drink Allow one to two glasses for guests on arrival; three to four with the meal (this is the upper limit and many guests will drink little or no

Below and opposite above **Good caterers offer increasingly international and eclectic menus. You might want to have a culinary theme to your reception, or little stalls offering different types of food, from dim sum to bowls of popcorn and sweets. At the other end of the spectrum, there's been a resurgence in the popularity of traditional, home-cooked fare such as fish and chips and bangers and mash.**

Opposite below **If champagne is beyond your budget, investigate the many sparkling wines on the market. You can reserve your sparkling wine for the speeches and toasts, serving other types of drink during the meal.**

alcohol); and a glass with the speeches and toasts. Champagne is the traditional wedding drink but it's expensive, so many couples serve a sparkling wine instead and reserve it for the speeches and toasts only. It's normal to serve red and white wine with a seated meal or buffet. Beer is often popular with younger guests. Punches can be cost-effective since the amount of alcohol used is fairly small. Pimm's is refreshing in summer, while mulled wine is warming in winter. Ask if you can order drink on a sale or return basis. Don't forget that lots of people will want soft drinks, particularly anyone who's driving. Water, fruit juice or non-alcoholic fruit punch, tea and coffee are always welcome. If you're trying to save money, you could provide the first couple of drinks then have a bar. Find out if your venue will let you provide your own wine and how much corkage they charge. If you fancy a day-trip over the Channel to buy your wine in France, this can be good value, too.

Toastmasters Some couples hire a toastmaster to act as a master of ceremonies and to ensure that the reception runs smoothly and to time. He can announce guests to their hosts as they arrive; when it's time for the meal to begin; the speeches and toasts; and the cutting of the cake. Toastmasters traditionally wear a very smart uniform including a tailcoat. If you book one, make sure he is a member of a recognized professional association. In the absence of a toastmaster, the best man assumes his duties.

Reception entertainment ideas

♥ A casino (with play money). ♥ A magician or illusionist. ♥ A caricaturist. ♥ Fireworks. ♥ Jugglers, fire eaters or stilt walkers. ♥ Releasing white doves.

The seating plan If you're having an informal buffet, you may want to let guests sit where they want. However, for a formal plated meal, a seating plan is a good idea since it avoids a chaotic scramble for places. Give yourself plenty of time to draw it up – it can be a bit of a game of musical chairs trying to get it right. Obviously, your aim is to put together people who'll enjoy each other's company. Some of your guests will already know each other. Otherwise, bear in mind a few guidelines. People of the same age are normally best together. Look for things that guests have in common – whether they have children, their jobs and their interests. Try for a mixture of extroverts and those who need drawing out, and for a balance of men and women. Work single people into the plan at an early stage so you don't end up using them as 'fillers'. Married couples should be on the same table, but not next to each other. Close family and older friends should be on tables close to the top table. The bride and groom usually take their seats last so that everyone can applaud them as they come in. The top table is also normally served with food first.

The seating plan itself is normally displayed on a large board at the entrance to the reception. The plan can be a simple printed list or you may want to make it into a feature, having it handwritten or decorated in some way. Another approach is to write guests' names and table numbers on little seating cards, with or without envelopes, and place these on a table for people to collect as they arrive. Alternatively, each card could be attached to a flower or favour (for more ideas for favours, see page 109).

The top table If your and/or your fiancé's parents have divorced and remarried, you'll have to decide whether you want them all on the top table. If there isn't room, you could have a table close by and seat step-parents at that. If one parent has remarried but the other has not, it's an idea to find an escort for the unmarried one to balance the table. If you're trying to work out a seating plan, remember that your and your fiancé's parents should be either side of you as on the traditional plan, with step-parents added on to either end as necessary, alternating between men and women.

Traditional top table seating plan Facing the top table:

chief bridesmaid	groom's father	bride's mother	groom	bride	bride's father	groom's mother	best man

Above left **These place cards have been threaded onto ribbon, which is used to tie up the napkins. A rose adds a final flourish.**

Centre left **At a large reception it may be impractical to make a special feature of place cards. However, if yours is a smaller gathering, you could attach the cards to little boxes of favours.**

Below left **This unusual and striking table setting has been created by using miniature galvanized buckets (available from florists) for individual flower arrangements. The silver finish of the buckets is the perfect foil for the green and white flowers and foliage.**

Above right **These napkin rings are made of wide satin ribbon, onto which rectangles of paper with guests' names have been stuck. Rosemary sprigs add colour and scent.**

Below right **Paper cones can be tied to the backs of chairs and filled with sweets or, as here, flowers and foliage.**

Table decorations Take your dress, flowers and attendants' outfits as the starting point for your colour scheme so everything works together. For tablecloths and napkins, white is the obvious choice and always looks chic, acting as a foil to other colours. However, pastels are pretty and green, red or gold would be good choices for a winter wedding. Once you've chosen the basics, think about other details: candles, table centrepieces, place cards, menus and flowers.

Hiring equipment Most reception venues supply tables, chairs, china and so on. Marquee companies and caterers may also be able to do so. Otherwise, you'll need to contact a catering-hire company. Plans for food and drink and the number of guests must be finalized before you place your order. Good hire companies will have basic lines and more decorative ranges to cater for different tastes and budgets. Your hire checklist may include the following: tables; chairs; glasses (red and

Below and below right **At this outdoor wedding reception, simple elements have been cleverly combined to spectacular effect. By using a mixture of cottage-garden flowers and herbs, limiting the colour palette to whites and creams and using the blooms *en masse*, a feeling of luxuriance and abundance has been created. The flowers have been arranged unpretentiously in glass vases, along with bowls of gooseberries, greengages and white currants. Tall candelabra punctuate the design, giving structure and height.**

white wineglasses, water glasses and jugs, champagne flutes and glasses for the bar if you're having one); cutlery; serving dishes and cutlery; tablecloths and napkins; and table accessories such as salt and pepper mills, vases and candlesticks. Get several quotations for comparison. Check delivery charges; whether equipment can be returned dirty or must be clean; breakage terms; whether you need to take out insurance; and payment conditions. Someone will have to take delivery of the equipment and make sure that it's all there.

Decoration ideas

Place cards

♥ Use gold or silver pen to write guests' names on glossy leaves. Try laurel, rhododendron or magnolia.

♥ Write or paint names on pale pebbles (from garden centres or DIY stores).

♥ Tie name tags to single, long-stemmed flowers, or to the stems of fruits such as pears, cherries or Cape gooseberries.

Tables

♥ Keep table centrepieces low enough for guests to be able to talk over them.

♥ Try pyramids of glossy red apples or citrus fruits. Sugar-frosted fruits look pretty – dip into lightly beaten egg white and roll in caster sugar.

♥ If you're on a tight budget, try a single orchid or lily in a simple vase on each table.

♥ Flowers, petals, slices of citrus fruit or candles floating in shallow bowls of water look magical.

♥ Tint caster sugar with food colouring (pink looks pretty) and place in little bowls to serve with coffee.

♥ Make fruits such as oranges, lemons and limes into candle holders. Cut a slice off the base so they stand upright, then a slice off the top. Scoop out some of the flesh and place a nightlight inside.

♥ Tie napkins with lengths of ivy, ribbon or raffia.

♥ Scatter rose petals over the tables.

♥ Place candles, surrounded by herbs, moss and other foliage, in terracotta pots.

♥ Stick thin candles into jars filled with sand, pebbles and shells for a seaside feel.

♥ Instead of laying out cutlery in the usual way, tie up knives, forks and spoons with pretty ribbon into a bundle at each place.

♥ Look for inexpensive small baskets, or jam jars or glass tumblers (which can be tied with ribbon). Fill with cottage-garden flowers for a rustic look.

Chairs

♥ Decorate chair backs with ribbon bows, sprigs of flowers or herbs, or cones or boxes of sweets.

Favours The idea of giving guests favours comes from Italy. Here, they are called *bomboniere* and usually consist of five sugared almonds, representing health, wealth, happiness, longevity and fertility. However, a favour can be any kind of little gift, edible or otherwise, and if you're feeling creative and have time on your hands, you could try making your own for a really personal touch.

Creative favour ideas

♥ Little homemade bags of greaseproof paper filled with jellybeans, Smarties or other small sweets.

♥ Soaps or scented candles.

♥ Cupcakes, iced and topped with crystallized flowers (take unsprayed, edible varieties, such as roses, pansies or marigolds, dip first in lightly beaten egg white, then in sugar and put on a cake rack to dry).

♥ Biscuits, perhaps iced with initials (your guests' or your own).

♥ Small envelopes filled with flower seeds (perhaps love-in-a-mist or forget-me-not) or a single bulb (such as a narcissus or tulip) and planting instructions.

♥ Squares or rounds of organza or net filled with sugared almonds and tied with pretty ribbon.

♥ Petit-four or cupcake cases filled with mints or chocolates.

♥ Tiny bunches of flowers.

♥ Miniature terracotta pots planted up with a single bulb or flower.

♥ Homemade mini-muffins.

♥ Whole strawberries or cherries, dipped in dark or white chocolate.

Opposite Sugared almonds, or dragées, are traditional wedding favours since nuts are an ancient symbol of fertility. Here, however, little cellophane cones have been filled with white jellybeans.

Below Favours don't have to be edible: these little boxes, tied with silver cord and decorated with fabric flowers, are filled with spring bulbs which guests can plant at home as a permanent memento of the day.

Below right Pretty boxes can also be used for giving guests a slice of wedding cake to take home.

Handmade favours are sure to be appreciated.

Left and below White paper bags filled with loose tea, tied with ribbon. These could be arranged in rows along bands of satin ribbon or piled on a table next to a vase of flowers.

Opposite above left Instead of giving edible favours, why not place a few favourite flower seeds into little envelopes?

Opposite above right Luxurious, embroidered-linen lavender sachets nestle in a tissue-lined box.

Opposite below right Layers of ribbon and a velvet flower turn this favour box into a work of art.

Opposite below left Bundles of sweets can be made with circles of cellophane, net or tulle and ribbon.

The cake Catering staff often encourage couples to cut the cake before the speeches so that they can take it away and prepare it to be served with coffee afterwards. Although this makes practical sense, the traditional order of events is for cake-cutting to follow the speeches, when everyone's eyes are on the couple.

Types of cake The classic wedding cake is a rich fruit mixture, made into three tiers (normally supported by little columns, though it's popular now to have them stacked) and covered with marzipan and white royal icing. Fruit cake keeps well and couples often preserve the top tier for their first anniversary or the christening of their first child. If you want to do this, remove the icing and marzipan, wrap the cake in greaseproof paper and store in an airtight tin in a cool, dark place. Re-ice the cake when you need it. It's also a nice idea to send small pieces of cake to people who can't attend the wedding.

Alternative ideas

♥ Chocolate, lemon, coffee or carrot cake, or plain Madeira. Remember that if you want an iced cake, the cake itself must be fairly firm so as not to collapse.

♥ French croquembouche, a spectacular pyramid of cream-filled choux-pastry buns topped with caramel or spun sugar. If you want one, find an expert to make it – croquembouche is difficult to make and has to be served very fresh.

♥ Ice-cream cake, pavlova, cheesecake or, to follow one sweet-toothed bride's example, three huge banoffee pies on a tiered cake stand.

♥ A miniature wedding cake for each guest (most practical for small weddings) or individual sponges served with a fruit coulis, crème anglaise or chocolate sauce in place of dessert.

♥ Individual cupcakes or tarts, topped with icing, crystallized flowers or berries.

Decoration The inspiration for your cake could come from any number of sources: you and your fiancé's shared interests; your wedding venue; the time of year; the flowers and colours you are using; and so on. You could have a cake made to look like a pile of wedding presents, a giant heart or bow, or perhaps an open book of love poetry. You could also take inspiration from your dress.

Saving money Using a professional can be pricey and, if your budget doesn't allow it, there are DIY decorations to try. If you know someone who is happy to make the cake but doesn't feel up to icing it, see if a professional will ice it plainly as a basis for your own embellishment. Alternatively, cover the cake in ready-to-roll fondant, on sale in most supermarkets. Keep decorations simple for the best effect. Try ribbon tied round the side of your cake like a sash, finished with a bow; fresh or crystallized flowers (see page 109); ready-made sugar decorations, from cake-supply companies; sugared almonds; or fresh fruit.

Opposite **Beautiful effects can be created by using fresh flowers for your cake decoration. Here, a traditional three-tiered cake has been covered in plain white icing and draped with roses, ivy and lily of the valley. A garland of ivy and a scattering of rose petals around the base of the cake make it a focal point at the reception.**

Below **Sprigs of lime-green bupleurum contrast with the pure white icing of this stacked wedding cake.**

notes

notes

....
....
....
....
....
....
....
....
....
....
....
....
....
....
....
....
....
....
....
....
....
....
....
....
....
....
....
....
....
....
....
....

notes

....
....
....
....
....
....
....
....
....
....
....
....
....
....
....
....
....
....
....
....
....
....
....
....
....
....
....
....
....

notes

notes

....
....
....
....
....
....
....
....
....
....
....
....
....
....
....
....
....
....
....
....
....
....
....
....
....
....
....
....

notes

The gift list

Wedding presents often last a lifetime, so give your gift list
plenty of time and thought.

The wedding gift list

If you've ever fantasized about being let loose in a store and allowed to buy whatever you want, your wedding gift list will seem like a dream come true. However, a gift list serves a practical purpose, too, saving you from 10-crystal-vases syndrome. It also makes life easy for your guests and they can be confident that they've bought you something you really want. On the other hand, a present isn't the ticket that earns your guests the right to attend your wedding and it's important that you don't appear to be greedy or asking for presents as a right. Although many stores provide cards detailing where a list is held to be enclosed with wedding invitations, it is not considered good etiquette to do so. Leave it up to your guests to ask about the list if they want to.

How lists work

You could make up your own list. However, more and more companies are offering a gift list service, from department stores to specialist shops (and there's nothing to stop you having a list at more than one place). There are also gift list companies which deal with a wide range of suppliers, giving you an enormous choice of products and brands. It's often possible to make your selection from a catalogue or the internet if you can't visit in person. Gift list services are free and all use a similar system: you go round the store with a form and make your selection, which is then

Left **Gift lists used to be geared towards helping couples to set up home together, providing them with household basics. However, now that many couples live together before getting married and have all the essentials, lists often focus more on decorative and luxury items, such as the exquisite silverware shown here.**

Below **Many stores offer gift wrapping and free delivery.**

computerized. Guests can order in person or over the phone and you are sent regular updates detailing who has bought what. Presents can be collected or are delivered, often in one go after the wedding. If presents are sent to your home before the wedding, check that your insurance covers them while you're on honeymoon. You may want them to be delivered to your parents or in-laws instead or arrange to receive them after your honeymoon.

What to choose A gift list used to help couples to set up home and consisted of household basics: bed linen, china and so on. However, if you live together already or have been married before, the basics are probably redundant. You may therefore want decorative items for your home or garden, or something special, such as wine or books. If you want to put expensive items on your list, some stores allow guests to buy part of a gift. You may also be able to put gift vouchers on your list. However, it's unacceptable to ask for money.

Wedding gift checklist Use our basic list, below and on the next page, as a starting point for your own tailor-made list.

Opposite **With stores full of desirable homeware, it can be hard to know where to begin when you're compiling a list. Start by thinking about your list in relation to the number of guests you're inviting. Don't put so many items on it that you're unlikely to get full sets of anything, and cover a broad price range so that no one feels they've got to spend more than they can afford.**

China

- [ ] Dinner plates
- [ ] Side plates
- [ ] Dessert plates
- [ ] Cereal bowls
- [ ] Dessert bowls
- [ ] Soup bowls
- [ ] Soup tureen
- [ ] Vegetable dishes
- [ ] Platters
- [ ] Sauce boat
- [ ] Jugs
- [ ] Butter dish
- [ ] Teapot
- [ ] Cups and saucers
- [ ] Cream/milk jug
- [ ] Sugar bowl
- [ ] Coffee cups and saucers
- [ ] Coffee pot
- [ ] Egg cups

Glassware

- [ ] Red wineglasses
- [ ] White wineglasses
- [ ] Champagne flutes
- [ ] Sherry glasses
- [ ] Liqueur glasses
- [ ] Brandy balloons
- [ ] Highballs
- [ ] Tumblers
- [ ] Decanter
- [ ] Fruit bowl
- [ ] Jugs
- [ ] Vases
- [ ] Corkscrew
- [ ] Ice bucket
- [ ] Wine rack

Cutlery

- [ ] Large knives
- [ ] Large forks
- [ ] Small knives
- [ ] Small forks
- [ ] Fish knives/forks
- [ ] Dessert spoons
- [ ] Soup spoons
- [ ] Teaspoons
- [ ] Tablespoons/ serving spoons
- [ ] Butter knives
- [ ] Salad servers
- [ ] Cake slice
- [ ] Cheese knife
- [ ] Fish slice
- [ ] Ladle

Linen

- [ ] Mattress cover
- [ ] Undersheets
- [ ] Sheets
- [ ] Blankets
- [ ] Pillows
- [ ] Pillowcases
- [ ] Duvet
- [ ] Duvet covers
- [ ] Valance
- [ ] Cushions
- [ ] Electric blanket
- [ ] Tablecloths
- [ ] Napkins
- [ ] Napkin rings
- [ ] Place mats
- [ ] Coasters
- [ ] Tea towels
- [ ] Hand towels
- [ ] Bath towels
- [ ] Bath sheets
- [ ] Bath mats
- [ ] Facecloths

Kitchenware

- [ ] Baking tins
- [ ] Baking trays
- [ ] Balloon whisk
- [ ] Blender

Gift list dos and don'ts

♥ Set up your list well before your wedding so that it's done by the time your invitations are sent out.

♥ Going round a shop taking endless decisions can be exhausting, so do it in a couple of trips if necessary.

♥ Make sure your list covers a broad price range.

♥ Don't make your list too long or you'll end up with incomplete sets.

♥ Check the availability of items – there's nothing worse than finding that your dinner service is about to be discontinued.

♥ Write your thank-yous as presents arrive, to save you a mountain of letters after your honeymoon. Letters should be personal and handwritten.

♥ Some guests will bring presents on the day. Ask someone to make sure they're safe and that cards are firmly stuck on presents (give them a roll of tape). Someone will have to take away the presents at the end of the reception.

Opposite **If you're having gifts delivered to your home before the wedding, make sure that your insurance covers them while you're away on honeymoon. It will also save lots of paperwork when you're back if you start writing thank-you letters as presents arrive.**

Opposite below right **The recent surge of interest in gardening means that garden furniture, pots, tools and even plants are making appearances on wedding lists.**

☐ Bread bin
☐ Bread board
☐ Bread knife
☐ Cafetière
☐ Candlesticks
☐ Carving knife
☐ Casserole
☐ Cheese board
☐ Chopping board
☐ Colander
☐ Double boiler
☐ Electric carving knife
☐ Electric hand whisk
☐ Espresso/ cappuccino maker
☐ Flan dish
☐ Food processor
☐ Frying pan
☐ Garlic press
☐ Griddle
☐ Jam pot/spoon
☐ Juicer

☐ Kettle
☐ Kitchen knives/ block
☐ Kitchen timer
☐ Kitchen tool set
☐ Knife sharpener
☐ Mixing bowls
☐ Mugs
☐ Nutcracker
☐ Omelette pan
☐ Oven gloves
☐ Pressure cooker
☐ Pudding basins
☐ Ramekins
☐ Roasting tin
☐ Rolling pin
☐ Salad bowl
☐ Salad spinner
☐ Salt and pepper mills
☐ Sandwich maker
☐ Saucepans
☐ Scales

☐ Scissors
☐ Sharpening steel
☐ Sieve
☐ Slow cooker
☐ Soufflé dish
☐ Spatulas
☐ Spice rack/jars
☐ Steamer
☐ Storage tins/jars
☐ Toaster
☐ Trays
☐ Trivet
☐ Wok
☐ Wooden spoons

House and garden
☐ Barbecue
☐ Bathroom scales
☐ Books
☐ Camcorder
☐ Clocks
☐ Cushions
☐ DIY tools

☐ Garden furniture
☐ Garden pots
☐ Garden tools
☐ Iron
☐ Ironing board
☐ Lamps
☐ Lawnmower
☐ Linen basket
☐ Luggage
☐ Microwave
☐ Mirrors
☐ Photo frames
☐ Picnic basket
☐ Pictures/paintings
☐ Radio
☐ Rugs
☐ Stepladder
☐ Stereo
☐ Throws
☐ TV/video
☐ Vacuum cleaner
☐ Wine

notes

notes

....
....
....
....
....
....
....
....
....
....
....
....
....
....
....
....
....
....
....
....
....
....
....
....
....
....
....
....
....
....
....

The honeymoon

After the whirlwind excitement of the wedding, your honeymoon
will come as a welcome opportunity to relax and be alone together.

The honeymoon Travel has become one of our favourite pastimes. People are going further afield and spending longer away than before, and honeymooners are no exception. Long-haul destinations are not as difficult or expensive to get to as they once were and there are good deals to be had if you do your research. However, don't overlook short-haul options, particularly if you don't have time for a two-week break. You could even stay on home soil – not exotic, perhaps, but no passport or tickets to remember, either.

The first night Ask your best man to make sure your cases are in your going-away car or go on to your hotel ahead of you. When you book your hotel, let them know you'll be newlyweds, as they may offer complimentary champagne, flowers or chocolates. Dashing off to catch a flight the morning after a wedding can be a stressful start to a honeymoon, so consider a two-night stay.

The trip By tradition the groom plans and pays for the honeymoon, though many couples make it a joint venture. If your fiancé wants to surprise you, persuade him at least to tell you whether to pack for hot or cold weather. Couples with demanding jobs may find it hard to get away for long enough to make a far-flung honeymoon worthwhile. There is, therefore, a trend towards deferred or two-part trips; perhaps a long weekend after the wedding, then a two-week trip a few months later. If you're short of time, don't try to pack in too much or travel too far. Above all, a honeymoon should be relaxing.

Honeymoon tips

- Set your budget before you visit the travel agent – brochures are seductive.
- Research your destination. Brochures present things in the best light and guidebooks or the internet will give you a more objective view.

Above left **Weddings abroad are increasingly popular. If you're getting married on a tropical beach, traditional wedding clothes won't look or feel right. Natural fibres such cotton or linen are cool and comfortable (silk can be surprisingly hot), but may not travel as well as fine synthetics. Pack your dress in tissue paper, stuffing the sleeves and bodice. Put in a waterproof zip-up bag then, ideally, in a hard suitcase. For the groom, a cotton or linen suit is ideal**

Travel with an established tour operator which is member of an association such as ABTA (the Association of British Travel Agents).

Allow plenty of time to change your name on your passport or arrange visas. Tell the travel agent whether you'll be travelling under your maiden or married name; your ticket and passport must tally.

You may need inoculations well before you travel. Ask your tour operator or GP.

Order foreign currency or traveller's cheques a couple of weeks before you go.

Arrange for your wedding gifts to be delivered to someone while you're away or ask for them to be held at the store and delivered when you're back.

Reconfirm all your travel details and flights before you go, and pick up your travel documents.

Take out travel insurance with the tour operator or an insurance company. If you're travelling within the EU, pick up an E111 form from the post office, which facilitates medical care in these countries.

Packing tips

A suitcase with wheels helps to prevent aching back and shoulders.

On a long flight planes can get chilly, so wear something warm and loose-fitting. Take off your shoes and drink lots of water.

♥ A hard case gives contents the best protection.

♥ Pack heavy items in the bottom of your case.

♥ Put your wash bag in a plastic bag in case of leaks, and decant toiletries into plastic travel bottles.

♥ Roll up T-shirts, socks, swimwear and underwear and use them to cushion delicate items.

♥ Take clothes in a limited colour palette so you can mix and match. Fabrics with Lycra travel well.

♥ Hang crumpled clothes in the bathroom, where the steam helps creases to drop out.

Beauty sense

♥ Drink lots of water to prevent dehydration on the plane, and go easy on alcohol.

♥ Wear sun protection with an SPF of at least 15. Don't forget lips, eyes and ears. Reapply cream liberally every couple of hours.

♥ If you're pale, try a self-tanner. Exfoliate and moisturize the skin before use, especially dry areas.

♥ Use alcohol-free perfume in the sun or it may change its smell and cause skin irritation.

♥ Take a rich conditioner to prevent your hair from becoming dry in sun, sea and chlorinated pools.

♥ Use plenty of moisturizer and after-sun lotion to rehydrate the skin.

♥ Useful make-up includes waterproof mascara, bronzing powder and lip colour with sunscreen.

Weddings abroad If the thought of a traditional wedding leaves you cold, marrying in an exotic destination may be the answer. There are often financial advantages, since a wedding abroad need not be more expensive than a honeymoon alone. Organizing it should be easier, too, because a tour operator will take care of all the arrangements and legal paperwork. Most major operators offer weddings around the world. You can get married on a beach, on safari, on the ski slopes, in hot-air balloons and even underwater. Perhaps best of all, you'll be spared that mad dash to the airport the morning after your wedding – you're already there.

❤ Talk to several tour operators to compare prices and service. Choose one which treats you as individuals and takes note of your wishes.

❤ For your wedding to be legal in this country, it must be legal in the country where it took place. Requirements around the world vary, so do check.

❤ Various documents, usually originals, are required a couple of months or so before travel. If you're divorced, these include the decree absolute.

❤ You may want to be accompanied by family and friends. Will you pay for them or ask them to pay for themselves? Some may be willing and able to pay, but don't put anyone who isn't under pressure.

❤ With a wedding abroad you won't have as much control over such things as catering and flowers as you would at home. Have realistic expectations.

❤ Check exactly what is included in your wedding package so you don't have any nasty surprises.

❤ Destinations have high and low seasons. Low season is cheaper, but check the weather forecast.

❤ Remember that at a popular resort you won't be the only couple getting married on the day.

❤ Build in time to acclimatize before your wedding. You may be jet-lagged and you'll be in a different culture, climate and time zone.

❤ Civil ceremonies are the norm for weddings abroad. A religious one may not be possible.

❤ Always take out insurance.

❤ Check in good time that your passport is still in date, whether you need a visa and what inoculations and/or medication are required.

tes

....
....
....
....
....
....
....
....
....
....
....
....
....
....
....
....
....
....
....
....
....
....
....
....
....
....
....

notes

re are many stockists
d suppliers of all
ngs wedding related.
ow is a selection of
ne of them.

URANCE

A Direct
45 3000762)
L Insurance
707 423800)
lesiastical Direct
00 336622)
kson Emms
18 9575491)

EDDING
ORDINATORS &
NSULTANTS

ernative Occasions
932 872115)
ricia Rogerson
771 655996)
bhan Craven-Robins
0 7481 4338)
dding Coordination
Marvellous Moments
789 267728)
w.coolwhite.com
0 7351 7899)

GAGEMENT RINGS

tional Association
Goldsmiths
0 7613 4445)
ormation line
45 6040165)

Asprey & Garrard
167 New Bond Street
London W1S 4AR
(020 7493 6767)
Boodle & Dunthorne
1 Sloane Street
London SW1X 9LA
(020 7235 0111)

128–130 Regent Street
London W1R 5FE
(020 7437 5050)

Also at Harrods
(020 7730 1234).

52 Eastgate Street
Chester CH1 1ES
(01244 326666)

1 King Street
Manchester M2 6AW
(0161 8339000)

Boodles House
Lord Street
Liverpool L2 9SQ
(0151 2272525)
Cartier
175–176 New Bond
  Street
London W1S 4RN
(020 7408 5700)
David Morris
180 New Bond Street
London W1S 4RL
(020 7499 2200)
Goldsmiths
(0800 465376)
Branches nationwide.
H Samuel
(0800 3894683)
Branches nationwide.

Mappin & Webb
170 Regent Street
London W1B 5BQ
(020 7478 8700)
Also branches
nationwide: call
020 7734 3801.
Michael Rose
3 Burlington Arcade
London W1J 0PW
(020 7493 0714)
Piaget
(020 7343 7240)
Stocked nationwide.
Tiffany
25 Old Bond Street
London W1S 4QB
(020 7409 2790)
**The Wedding Ring
Company**
(01707 255050)
Stocked nationwide.

HEN & STAG PARTIES

Acorn Activities
(01432 830083)
Nationwide.
Action Events
(01892 519585)
South-East England
and northern France.
Activity Superstore
(01799 526526)
Nationwide.
**The Evening
Entertainment Company**
(0800 3285628)
Nationwide.
Freedom Limited
(0870 7875959)
Nationwide.

Red Letter Days
(020 8442 2001)
Nationwide.

STATIONERY

These companies offer
a mail-order service
unless stated.

Adrienne Kerr Designs
(0131 3325393)
Amelia Essex
(020 8858 1701)
Blue Tomatoes
(0151 6253924)
Catfish Cards
(01273 483935)
**Celtic Wedding
Stationery**
(00 353 12877378)
Chris Peake Stationery
(02920 222425)
Debenhams
(0870 2424555)
Josie Designs
(01743 249488)
Marks & Spencer
(01925 858502)
The Medieval Scribe
(01580 211383)
Old'n'Ugly Weddings
(02380 207759)
Colour caricatures of
the bride and groom.
Olivia Stationery
(01326 373649)
**Smythson of
Bond Street**
40 New Bond Street
London W1S 2DE
Call 08705 211311 for
mail order.

W H Smith
(01793 695195)
Personalized stationery
in-store only, at
branches nationwide.
The Wren Press
26 Chelsea Wharf
15 Lots Road
London SW10 0QJ
(020 7351 5887)

CALLIGRAPHY

Studio C Calligraphy
(01736 794113)
Mail order.

CRÈCHE SERVICES

Bubbles
(01245 464364)
**The Wedding
Crèche Service**
(01483 202490)

BRIDAL FASHION

Many designers and
shops operate on an
appointment-only
basis (this is why
addresses aren't
given in some cases).
It's wise to call to check
before you visit.

DESIGNERS & LABELS

Alan Hannah
(020 8882 0007)
Stocked nationwide.

Alfred Angelo
(01908 262626)
Stocked nationwide.
Allison Blake
(020 7732 9322)
Stocked nationwide.
Amanda Wakeley
80 Fulham Road
London SW3 6HR
(020 7590 9105)
Call 020 7471 8821
with bridalwear
enquiries.

Also at Regalia, Troon
(01292 312162); The
Bridal House of Chester
(01244 340707); and
The Wedding Dress at
Harrods (020 7225 5933).
Angela Stone
257 New King's Road
London SW6 4RB
(020 7371 5199)
Also mail order.
Angela Vickers
Nottingham
(0115 9415616)
Anita Massarella Design
490 Harrogate Road
Leeds LS17 6DL
(0113 2687783)
Anna Belinda Couture
6 Gloucester Street
Oxford OX1 2BN
(01865 246806)
Anna Christina Couture
(020 8527 7001)
Stocked nationwide.
Basia Zarzycka
52 Sloane Square
London SW1W 8AX
(020 7730 1660)

Berkertex Bride
(01476 593311)
Branches nationwide,
including a factory
shop in Grantham.
Blue
Cardiff
(029 2062 4477)
Also stocked
nationwide.
Blue Strawberry
(020 8300 6793)
Stocked nationwide.
Bridgette Moore Bridal
35 Upper Camden
 Street
Dublin 2
Ireland
(00 353 14755399)
Buttercup Couture
56 St Benedicts Street
Norwich
Norfolk NR2 4AR
(01603 760219)
Also stocked
nationwide.
By Storm
11 Chiltern Street
London W1N 1HB
(020 7224 7888)

The Cottage
156 Milngavie Road
Glasgow G61 3EA
(0141 9428900)
Caroline Holmes
176 Walton Street
London SW3 2JL
(020 7823 7678)

**Caroline Parkes
Bridal Design**
www.caroline
 parkes.com
Stocked nationwide.
Catherine Davighi
121 Adnitt Road
Northampton
NN1 4NQ
(01604 604122)
Also stocked
nationwide.
Catherine Walker
46 Fulham Road
London SW3 6HH
(020 7581 8811)
Christiana Couture
53 Moreton Street
London SW1V 2NY
(020 7976 5252)
Also diffusion range
stocked at Caroline
Castigliano shops.
David Fielden
London
(020 7351 0067)
Also stocked
nationwide.
Dizzie Lizzie Couture
(01803 296197)
Stocked nationwide.
Donna Salado
28–30 Abington Grov
Northampton
NN1 4QX
(01604 792869)
Also stocked
nationwide.
Droopy & Browns
99 St Martins Lane
London WC2N 4AZ
(020 7379 4514)

Droopy & Browns
21 Stonegate
York YO1 8AW
(01904 621458)
Eleni Bridal
London
(020 8886 7511)
Also stocked
nationwide.
Elizabeth Todd
Chiltern Street
London W1M 1HB
(020 7224 2773)
Ellis Bridals
(020 8888 8833)
Stocked nationwide.
Eternity Bridal
(01423 565444)
Stocked nationwide.
Evangeline Rose
5a Church Street
Godalming
Surrey GU7 1EL
(01483 415199)
Forever Yours
International
(01132 578111)
Stocked nationwide.
Hayley J
High Street
Shrewsbury
Shropshire SY1 1SP
(01743 235140)
Also stocked
nationwide.
Helen Marina
(020 8361 3777)
Stocked nationwide.
Hollywood Dreams
(020 8801 9797)
Stocked nationwide.
Ian Stuart International
(01908 615599)
Stocked nationwide.

Jacqueline Hogan
640 Fulham Road
London SW6 5RT
(020 7731 0911)
Jasper Conran at
The Wedding Shop
171 Fulham Road
London SW3 6JW
(020 7838 0171)
Jenny Burgess
London
(020 8941 7642)
Jenny Packham for
Mori Lee
(01476 591306)
Stocked nationwide.
Jenny Tyler
44 High Street
Bridgnorth Road
Much Wenlock
Shropshire TF13 6AD
(01952 728198)
Jessica McClintock
(020 8908 2690)
Stocked nationwide.
Judy Mott
Studio 8
Sussex Mews
The Pantiles
Royal Tunbridge Wells
Kent TN2 5QJ
(01892 510107)
Juliet Poyser
54–58 Tanner Street
London SE1 3PH
(020 7403 4377)
Kelsey Rose
(020 8888 8833)
Stocked nationwide.
Lila Lace
89 Hospital Street
Nantwich
Cheshire CW5 5RU
(01270 628943)

Louisa Scott
London
(020 7565 4100)
Louise Hamlin-Wright
Ashford
(01233 712868)
Louise Selby
Kew
(020 8948 8681)
Lyn-Mar
(00 353 40557737)
Stocked nationwide
and in Ireland.
Maggie Sottero
(0151 3559525)
Stocked nationwide.
Margaret Lee
(01702 616180)
Stocked nationwide.
Mirror Mirror
37 Park Road
London N8 8TE
(020 8348 2113)
Mori Lee
(01476 591306)
Stocked nationwide.
Neil Cunningham
28 Sackville Street
London W1S 3DU
(020 7437 5793)
Nicki Hill
5 The Square
Botley
Southampton
SO30 2EA
(01489 785942)
Oceanna by
Helen Marina
(020 8361 3777)
Stocked nationwide.

One & Only
81 Newton Road
Mumbles
Swansea SA3 4UD
(01792 361477)
Also stocked
nationwide.
Papillon
(020 8345 6725)
Stocked nationwide.
Peter Brandon Couture
(01604 792849)
Stocked nationwide.
Phillipa Lepley
494 Fulham Road
London SW6 5NH
(020 7386 0927)
Also stocked
nationwide.
Pretty Maids
5 Northampton Street
Leicester LE1 1PA
(0116 2549636)
Pronovias
(01254 679505)
Stocked nationwide.
Pronuptia Bridal
95 Hatton Garden
London EC1N 8NX
(020 7419 9014)
Branches nationwide.
Rena Koh
(0131 2258955)
Stocked nationwide.
Ritva Westenius
28 Connaught Street
London W2 2AF
(020 7706 0708)
Also stocked
nationwide.
Robinson Valentine
4 Hornton Place
London W8 4LZ
(020 7937 2900)

Romantica of Devon
(01884 860728)
Stocked nationwide.
Ronald Joyce, **Dante**,
Victoria Jane and **Rojo**
by Ronald Joyce
(020 7636 8989)
Stocked nationwide.
Sallie Bee
1172 Stratford Road
Hall Green
Birmingham B28 8AF
(0121 7786066)
Also stocked
nationwide.
Sassi Holford
6 The Bridge
Taunton
Somerset TA1 1UG
(01823 256308)
Also stocked
nationwide.
Sharon Bowen
Design Studio
Chester and London
(01260 271269)
Sharon Hoey
19 Upper Mount Street
Dublin 2
Ireland
(00 353 16762772)
Also stocked
nationwide.
Shelagh M
Wales
(01978 661008)
Also stocked
nationwide.
Sincerity
(01908 615511)
Stocked nationwide.

SoieMême
76 Belsize Park Gardens
London NW3 4NG
(020 7483 3843)
Sophie English
68a Rochester Row
London SW1P 1JU
(020 7828 9007)
Also stocked
nationwide.
Sposa Bella
(0121 7081841)
Stocked nationwide.
Stevies Gowns and
Athena Maria
(020 8803 8084)
Stocked nationwide.
Stewart Parvin
London
Call 020 7838 9808 for
couture.
Call 020 7235 1125 for
stockists nationwide.
Suzanne Glenton
42 Queenstown Road
London SW8 3RY
(020 7978 1010)
Suzanne Neville
44 High Street
Harrow-on-the-Hill
Middlesex HA1 3LL
(020 8423 3161)
Tracy Connop
(020 7323 1507)
Stocked nationwide.
Vera Wang at
The Wedding Shop
171 Fulham Road
London SW3 6JW
(020 7838 0171)
The White Rose
Collection
(020 7323 1507)
Stocked nationwide.

The Wizard of Gos
London
(020 7938 1025)
Also stocked
nationwide.

SHOPS

Affaires de Femme
31 Bedford Place
Southampton
SO15 2DG
(02380 236616)
Andrea Bambridge
64 Goodramgate
York YO1 7LF
(01904 640046)
Also own-label designs.
Aphrodite
1 The Cobbles
High Street
Bletchingley
Surrey RH1 4PB
(01883 743293)

23 King Street
Knutsford
Cheshire WA16 6DW
(01565 631000)
Aristocrats of Chester
St Werburgh Chambers
Godstall Lane
Chester CH1 1LH
(01244 317587)
Bell'Amore
240–242 Broadway
Bexley Heath
Kent DA6 8AS
(020 8298 1978)

Bellissima
Holcombe Mews
403 Bolton Road West
Holcombe Brook
Bury
Lancashire BL0 9RN
(01204 888025)
Bhs
(020 7262 3288)
Branches nationwide.
The Bridal House
of Chester
66–68 Northgate Stree
Chester CH1 2HT
(01244 340707)
The Bridal Path
222 Childwall Road
Liverpool L15 6UY
(0151 7220006)
The Bridal Room
31 Sun Street
Hitchin
Hertfordshire SG5 1AH
(01462 432889)
Bride To Be of Oxford
22 The Parade
Oxford Road
Kidlington
Oxfordshire OX5 1DB
(01865 376076)
Brides of Cheshire
The Old Shop
Aston-By-Budworth
nr Northwich
Cheshire CW9 6LT
(01565 733267)
Caroline Castigliano
62 Berners Street
London W1T 3NQ
(020 7636 8212)

6 Waterloo Place
Edinburgh EH1 3BG
(0131 5583355)

Caroline Castigliano
0 Tunsgate
Guildford
Surrey GU1 3QT
(01483 449994)

0 Water Lane
Wilmslow
Cheshire SK9 5AA
(01625 536262)
And branches. Also
own-label designs.

Chanticleer
1 Regent Street
Cheltenham
Gloucestershire
GL50 1HE
(01242 226502)
Also own-label designs.

Cherubs
6 High Road
Balby
Doncaster DN4 0PL
(01302 858261)

Complicité La Fete
-10 Maid Marian Way
Nottingham NG1 6HS
(115 9580600)

Confetti & Lace
Lakeside Shopping
Centre
West Thurrock
Grays
Essex RN16 1ZL
(1708 890353)

8 Catherine Street
Salisbury
Wiltshire SP1 2DA
(1722 329810)

Confetti & Lace
Unit 6
Historic Courtyard
Wilton Shopping
   Village
Wilton
Salisbury
Wiltshire SP2 0RS
(01722 742244)

16 The Broadwalk
North Street
Chichester
West Sussex PO19 1AR
(01243 531131)

4 Woolmead Walk
Farnham
Surrey GU9 7SH
(01252 722794)

The Cotswold
Frock Shop
3 Talbot Court
Stow-on-the-Wold
Gloucestershire
GL54 1BQ
(01451 832309)

De Stafford
21 Exchequer Street
Dublin 2
Ireland
(00 353 16798817)
Also own-label designs.

Diana Gray of Chester
11a Upper Northgate
   Street
Chester CH1 4EE
(01244 378220)

Eleganza Sposa
117 Quarry Street
Hamilton
South Lanarkshire
ML3 7DR
(01698 303050)

Elizabeth of York
12 Blake Street
York YO1 2QG
(01904 658600)

Emma Roy of Edinburgh
31–33 Leith Street
Edinburgh EH1 3AT
(0131 5572875)

Fripperies Wedding
Shoppe
2–3 Cloth Hall
5 North Street
Headcorn
Kent CN27 9NN
(01622 891844)

Grace & Lace
2 Canbridge Way
Chelmsford
Essex CM2 0BX
(01245 347347)

46 St Botolphs Street
Colchester
Essex CO2 7EB
(01206 563000)

Gypsophila
205–207 Bacup Road
Rawtenstall
Rossendale
Lancashire BB4 7NW
(01706 213242)

House of Fraser
(020 7963 2236)
Branches nationwide.

Jane of Cambridge
17–19 Sussex Street
Cambridge CB1 1PA
(01223 314455)

Jenners
47 Princes Street
Edinburgh ED2 2YJ
(0131 2252442)

Liberty
210–220 Regent Street
London W1B 5AH
(020 7734 1234)

The London Designer
Bridal Room
Dickins & Jones
224–244 Regent Street
London W1B 3AD
(020 7434 3966)

Losners
232 Stamford Hill
London N16 6TT
(020 8800 7466)

12–14 Victoria Street
St Albans
Hertfordshire AL1 3JB
(01727 833823)

Love In A Mist
9 Hall Street
Long Melford
Sudbury
Suffolk CO10 9JG
(01787 881388)

Maid in Heaven
4–5 Thame House
Castle Street
High Wycombe
Buckinghamshire
HP13 6RZ
(01494 474363)

Margot Raybould
16 Upper Green
Tettenhall
Wolverhampton
WV6 8QH
(01902 750933)

Marian Gale
8 The Mall
Donnybrook
Dublin 4
Ireland
(00 353 12697467)
Also own-label designs.

Miss Bush Bridalwear
Ye Olde Shoppe
High Street
Ripley
Surrey G23 6AZ
(01483 222815)

Mon Chéri
5 Norman Way
Over
Cambridge CB4 5QE
(01954 232102)

Morgan Davies
62 Cross Street
London N1 2BA
(020 7354 3414)

The Pantiles Bride
34 The Pantiles
Royal Tunbridge Wells
Kent TN2 5TN
(01892 514515)

Prettymades
341 Lymington Road
Highcliffe-on-Sea
Christchurch
Dorset BH23 5EG
(01425 276688)
Also own-label designs.

Regalia
46 Church Street
Troon
Ayrshire KA10 6AU
(01292 312162)

Roberta Buchan
176 Hope Street
Glasgow G2 2TU
(0141 3326060)

Selfridges
400 Oxford Street
London W1A 1AB
(020 7629 1234)

Sugared Almonds
12 Skipton Road
Earby
Lancashire BB18 6PX
(01282 844800)

Surrey Brides
52 Church Street
Weybridge
Surrey KT13 8DP
(01932 846812)

Sweet Dreams
24 Chertsey Street
Guildford
Surrey GU1 4HD
(01483 537123)

Taftas
19 Baddow Road
Chelmsford
Essex CM2 0BX
(01245 265527)

Tickled Pink
2–4 Manor Road
Hatfield
Doncaster DN7 6SB
(01302 842234)

The Wedding Centre
Maple House
21–23 Little Marlow
    Road
Marlow
Buckinghamshire
SL7 1HA
(01628 478888)

The Wedding Company
of Warwick
76 Smith Street
Warwick CV34 4HU
(01926 494929)

Wedding Days
of Cheltenham
First Floor
Cambray House
33 Cambray Place
Cheltenham
Gloucestershire
GL50 1JP
(01242 224965)

The Wedding Dress
at Harrods
87–135 Brompton
    Road
Knightsbridge
London SW1X 7XL
(020 7225 5933)

The Wedding Shop
171 Fulham Road
London SW3 6JW
(020 7838 0171)

37 Blandford Street
London W1V 7HB
(020 7935 6502)

Also at Liberty
(020 7573 9652).

The Wedding Studio
59 Queen's Road
Weybridge
Surrey KT13 9UQ
(01932 841066)

White Chapel
343 Ecclesall Road
Sheffield S11 8PF
(0114 2671111)

HIRE & NEARLY NEW

Belles
20 Guildford Road
Woking
Surrey GU22 7PX
(01483 715858)

The Bridal Gown
Exchange
The Mill House
Badger
Burnhill Green
Wolverhampton
WV6 7JU
(01746 783066)

Cocoa Designs
9 Clarence Parade
Cheltenham
Gloucestershire
GL50 3NY
(01242 233588)
Antique lace dresses.

Déjà Vu
34 Oak Road
Cobham
Surrey KT11 3BA
(01932 860461)

Pronuptia
(01273 563006)
Branches nationwide.

The Wedding Centre
30 St Mary's Place
Newcastle upon Tyne
NE1 7PQ
(0191 2325295)

SMALL SIZES

Weston Wedding Petite
Odell House
11 High Street
Newport Pagnell
Buckinghamshire
MK16 8AR
(01908 216688)
Also stocked
nationwide.

LARGE SIZES

The companies below
produce ready-to-wear
dresses in large sizes.
Call for your nearest
stockist.

Alfred Angelo
(01908 262626)
Berkertex Bride
(01476 593311)
Diva by Paloma Blanca
(01274 598380)
Eternity Bridal
(01423 565444)
Forever Yours
International
(01132 578111)
Ian Stuart International
(01908 615599)
Jenny Packham for
Mori Lee
(01476 591306)
Jessica McClintock
(020 8908 2690)
Papillon
(020 8345 6725)
Ronald Joyce
(020 7636 8989)
Sincerity
(01908 615511)
Stardust by Sallie Bee
(0121 7786066)

ATTENDANTS

Ian Hannah
(020 8882 0007)
Stocked nationwide;
adult and young
bridesmaids.

Berkertex Bride
(01476 593311)
Branches nationwide;
adult and young
bridesmaids.
Bhs
(020 7262 3288)
Branches nationwide;
young bridesmaids
and pageboys.
Fairy Tales Bridal
Boutique
The Square
Angmering
West Sussex BN16 4EA
(01903 787879)
Also mail order.
Jenny Tyler
44 High Street
Bridgnorth Road
Much Wenlock
Shropshire TF13 6AD
(01952 728198)
Adult and young
bridesmaids and
pageboys.
Jessica McClintock
(020 8908 2690)
Stocked nationwide.
Adult and young
bridesmaids.
Jim Hjelm Occasions
(0800 3281531)
Stocked nationwide.
Adult bridesmaids.
Little Wings
(020 7243 3840)
Mail order; fairy outfits
for young bridesmaids.
Lou Lou
(01322 440225)
Stocked nationwide.
Adult and young
bridesmaids.

Monsoon
(020 7313 3000)
Branches nationwide.
Dresses suitable for
adult and young
bridesmaids.
Nicki Hill
5 The Square
Botley
Southampton
SO30 2EA
(01489 785942)
Also stocked
nationwide; adult and
young bridesmaids
and pageboys.
Olive
(01460 55665)
Stocked nationwide.
Adult and young
bridesmaids; pageboys.
Pretty Maids
5 Northampton Street
Leicester LE1 1PA
(0116 2549636)
Adult and young
bridesmaids and
pageboys.
Prettymades
341 Lymington Road
Highcliffe-on-Sea
Christchurch
Dorset BH23 5EG
(01425 276688)
Also mail order. Adult
and young
bridesmaids and
pageboys.
Ronald Joyce
(020 7636 8989)
Stocked nationwide;
adult and young
bridesmaids.

Serafina
2 Michael Road
London SW6 2ER
(020 7731 5215)
Adult and young
bridesmaids and
pageboys.
Virgin Bride
The Grand Buildings
Northumberland
  Avenue
London WC2N 5EJ
(020 7321 0866)
Adult and young
bridesmaids and
pageboys.
Watters & Watters
www.watters.com
Stocked nationwide;
adult bridesmaids.

DRESSMAKING

Butterick/Vogue
(02392 486221)
Dress patterns.
Can provide a list
of dressmakers in
your area.

DRY-CLEANING

The Dry-cleaning
Information Bureau
(020 8863 8658)
Can recommend dry-
cleaners in your area.

DRESS STORAGE

The Empty Box
Company
(01306 740193)
Mail order.

Restore Products
(0161 9280020)
Mail order.

HISTORICAL COSTUME HIRE

Angels
119 Shaftesbury
   Avenue
London WC2H 8AE
(020 7836 5678)
Costume Company
Tyn-Y-Bwlch
Glan-Yr-Afon
Corwen
Denbighshire
LR21 0HE
(01490 460337)
Nationwide service.
The Royal Exchange
Costume Hire
Manchester
(0161 9326800)
By appointment only.

VEILS

The Honiton Lace Shop
44 High Street
Honiton
Devon EX14 1PJ
(01404 42416)
Also mail order.
Irresistible
West Sussex
(01403 871449)
Also mail order.
Jenny Burgess
(020 8941 7642)
Mail order.
Joyce Jackson
(01745 343689)
Stocked nationwide.

Richard Designs
(01353 661600)
Stocked nationwide.

Many companies
providing accessories,
listed below, operate
on an appointment-
only basis; call to check.

HEADDRESSES & HAIR DECORATIONS

Accessorize
(020 7313 3000)
Branches nationwide.
Bijoux Heart
(01709 363318)
Mail order.
Blossom
Unit 3, Itchel Home Farm
Itchel Lane
Crondall, Farnham
Surrey GU10 5PT
(01252 851733)
Also mail order.
Butler & Wilson
20 South Molton Street
London W1K 5QU
(020 7409 2955)

189 Fulham Road
London SW3 6JN
(020 7352 3045)
Daisy Nook Designs
26 Copythorne Road
Brixham
Devon TQ5 8QE
(01803 859255)
Mail order.
Devoré
London
(020 7608 0542)
Also mail order.

Elizabeth Edema
London
(020 7229 2564)
Halo
(01283 704305)
Stocked nationwide.
Heidi Headwear
(01243 827216)
Stocked nationwide.
Irresistible
West Sussex
(01403 871449)
By appointment and
mail order.
Jenny Wicks
Manchester
(0161 4346855)
Stocked nationwide
and mail order.
Johnny Loves Rosie
(020 7375 3574)
Stocked nationwide
and mail order.
Josie Baird Tiaras
at Harrods
87–135 Brompton
   Road
Knightsbridge
London SW1X 7XL
(020 7730 1234)
Leigh-Anne McCague at
Fripperies Wedding
Shoppe
2–3 Cloth Hall
5 North Street
Headcorn
Kent CN27 9NN
(01622 890922)
Also mail order.
Malcolm Morris
London
(020 7916 8060)

Petals International
(01132 660388)
Stocked nationwide.
Polly Edwards
(01903 882127)
Stocked nationwide.
Serendipity
(01342 713828)
Stocked nationwide
and mail order.
Slim Barrett
London
(020 7354 9393)
Mail order.
The Tiara Gallery
London
(020 7729 7350)

HATS

Accessorize
(020 7313 3000)
Branches nationwide.
Debenhams
(020 7408 4444)
Branches nationwide.
Edwina Ibbotson
45 Queenstown Road
London SW8 3RG
(020 7498 5390)
Emma Carlow
London
(020 7737 1042)
Felicity Hat Hire
(01772 742428)
Branches nationwide.
Frederick Fox
17 Avery Row
London W1K 4BF
(020 7629 5706)
Also stocked
nationwide.

Gabriela Ligenza
5 Ellis Street
London SW1X 9AL
(020 7730 2200)
Herald & Heart Hatters
131 St Philip Street
London SW8 3SS
(020 7627 2414)
Herbert Johnson
54 St James's Street
London SW1A 1JT
(020 7408 1174)
House of Fraser
(020 7963 2236)
Branches nationwide.
Marks & Spencer
(020 7935 4422)
Branches nationwide.
Nigel Rayment
Luton
(01582 481263)
Philip Somerville
38 Chiltern Street
London W1U 7QL
(020 7224 1517)
Philip Treacy
59 Elizabeth Street
London SW1W 9PJ
(020 7824 8787)
Rachel Skinner
London
020 7209 0066)
Rachel Trevor-Morgan
London
020 7839 8927)
Stephen Jones
36 Great Queen Street
London WC2B 5AA
020 7242 0770)
Sue Levene
London
020 7724 7965)

Susy Krakowski
20 Altrincham Road
Wilmslow
Cheshire SK9 5ND
(01625 535365)
Also stocked
nationwide.
Sylvia Fletcher at
James Lock & Co
6 St James's Street
London SW1A 1EF
(020 7930 5849)

SHOES

Anello & Davide
47 Beauchamp Place
London SW3 1NX
(020 7225 2468)
Benjamin Walk
Bridal Shoes
(01933 682011)
Stocked nationwide
and mail order.
Danceland Shoe
Company
(01782 635515)
Mail order.
Emma Hope
53 Sloane Square
London SW1W 8AX
(020 7259 9566)

207 Westbourne Grove
London W11 2SE
(020 7313 7493)
Fenaroli for Regalia
www.fenaroli.com
Stocked nationwide.
French Sole
6 Ellis Street
London SW1 9AL
(020 7730 3779)
Also mail order.

Gamba
3 Garrick Street
London WC2E 9AR
(020 7437 0704)
Also stocked
nationwide. Call
020 8903 8177 for
your nearest stockist.
Hanna Goldman Shoes
London
(020 7739 2690)
HKE
(01323 728988)
Stocked nationwide
and mail order.
Ivory Shoes
104 New Bond Street
London W1Y 9LG
(020 7408 1266)
Also mail order.
Kate Pennington
London
(020 8203 2647)
Also mail order.
Melbo Shoes
London
(020 8505 2626)
Also mail order.
Nine to Elleven
Footwear & Clothing
(01420 561947)
Larger sizes; mail order.
Rainbow Club
(01392 207030)
Stocked nationwide.
Shades
(01132 438067)
Stocked nationwide.

SHOE DYEING

The companies below
will dye their own
shoes and, sometimes,
bags. For phone
numbers, see above.

Danceland
HKE
Ivory
Rainbow Club
Shades

GARTERS

Arsenic & Old Lace
(01244 811721)
Mail order; also lucky
horseshoes.
E & P Designs
(01733 840455)
Stocked nationwide.
HKE
(01323 728988)
Stocked nationwide
and mail order.

BAGS

Accessorize
(020 7313 3000)
Branches nationwide.
Bhs
(020 7262 3288)
Branches nationwide.
Clare Musgrove
(01902 753533)
Stocked nationwide.
Debenhams
(020 7408 4444)
Branches nationwide.

Dollargrand
(020 7794 3028)
Stocked nationwide.
E & P Designs, as above
HKE, as above
Ivory, as above
Rainbow Club, as above
Shades, as above

GLOVES

Cornelia James
45 Maddox Street
London W1S 2PE
(020 7499 9423)
By appointment. Also
stocked nationwide.
Dents
(01985 212291)
Stocked nationwide.
E & P Designs
(01733 840455)
Stocked nationwide.
HKE
(01323 728988)
Stocked nationwide
and mail order.

GROOMS

Allan Kelly
16 East Street
Bromley
Kent DR1 1QU
(020 8460 6811)
Anthony Formalwear
53 High Street
Billericay
Essex CM12 9AX
(01277 651140)
Darcy Design
(01323 645697)
Mail order.

Fantasy Waistcoats
(0121 3532848)
Mail order.
Favourbrook
55 Jermyn Street
London SW1Y 6LX
(020 7491 2337)
Formal Affair
(0800 9178092)
Stores in Wales and
the Midlands.
Greenwoods Menswear
(01943 876100)
Stores nationwide.
Heaphys
(0808 1002498)
Stores in the Midlands.
The Kilt Hire Company
54–56 Haymarket
Terrace
Edinburgh EH12 5LA
(0800 0185458)
Lords Formal Wear
1st Floor
Cabot Place East
Canary Wharf
London E14 5QT
(020 7363 1033)
Masterhand
(01480 460400)
Stocked nationwide.
Moss Bros
(020 7447 7200)
Stores nationwide.
Peter Posh
Unit D3
Stafford Park 11
Telford
Shropshire TF3 3AY
(08702 201781)
Piscador
(020 8898 3666)
Stocked nationwide.

Pronuptia
(01273 563006)
Branches nationwide.
Tux 'N' Tails by Losners
(020 8800 9281)
Stores in the Home
Counties.
Virgin Bride
The Grand Buildings
Northumberland
Avenue
London WC2N 5EJ
(020 7321 0866)
Youngs Hire at Suits You
(020 8327 3005)
Stores nationwide.

SPAS

**The Aveda Concept
Salon and Urban Retreat
at Harvey Nichols**
London
(020 7201 8610)
Leeds
(0113 2440212)
**The Bath House at The
Royal Crescent Hotel**
Bath
(01225 8233333)
**The Berkeley Health
Club and Spa**
London
(020 7235 6000)
Cedar Falls Health Farm
Somerset
(01823 433233)
**Champneys Health
Resort**
Hertfordshire
(01442 291000)
**Chewton Glen Health
and Country Club**
Hampshire
(01425 277674)

The Dorchester Spa
London
(020 7629 8888)
Elemis Day Spa
London
(020 7499 4995)
**Elizabeth Arden
Red Door Hair and
Beauty Spa**
London
(020 7629 4488)
Forest Mere
Hampshire
(01428 722051)
**Grayshott Hall Health
Fitness Retreat**
Surrey
(01428 604331)
**Henlow Grange
Health Farm**
Bedfordshire
(01462 811111)
**Ragdale Hall Health
Hydro**
Leicestershire
(01664 434831)
St David's Hotel and Spa
Cardiff
(02920 313084)
The Sanctuary
London
(08700 630300)
Springs Health Farm
Leicestershire
(01530 273873)
Stobo Castle Health Spa
Peebleshire
(01721 760249)

BEAUTY SALONS

Call for details of your nearest salon.

Clarins
(020 7307 6700)
Decleor
(020 7262 0403)
Elemis
(020 8954 8033)
E'SPA
(01252 741600)
Gatineau
(01753 620881)
Thalgo
(020 7512 0872)

HAIR

Call 02392 812233 to find a salon near you recommended by *The Good Salon Guide*.
www.goodsalon
    guide.co.uk

Kérastase Consultant Salons
(0800 3164400)
Salons nationwide.
L'Oréal Premium Hair Salons
(0800 0726699)
Salons nationwide.
Toni & Guy Salons
(020 7440 6660)
Salons nationwide.
Umberto Giannini
(01384 444771)
Salons in the Midlands.
Wella
(0870 5775544)
Salons nationwide.

RELIGIOUS & CIVIL WEDDINGS

The organizations below can offer help and advice.

Baptist Union
(01235 517700)
The British Humanist Association
(020 7430 0908)
Catholic Enquiry Office
(020 8458 3316)
Church of England Enquiry Centre
(020 7898 1000)
Church of Scotland Office
(0131 2255722)
Greek Orthodox Church Information
(020 7723 4787)
Institute of Indian Culture
(020 7381 3086)
Jewish Marriage Council
(020 8203 6311)
Marriage Care
(020 7243 1898)
Advice on Catholic marriage.
Methodist Church Press Office
(020 7467 5128)
Methodist Church
(020 7222 8010)
Muslim Information Centre
(020 7272 5170)
National Council of Hindu Temples
(01923 856269)

Scottish Episcopal Church
(0131 2256357)
Sikh Community Care Project
(020 8558 3199)
United Reformed Church
(020 7916 2020)

General Register Office for England and Wales
(0151 4714200)
Provides a full list of licensed civil venues for a small fee. Call 0151 4714817 for credit-card payments.
**www.registeroffice
    weddings.com**
The official register-office website. Listings of local register offices, plus useful wedding information.
General Register Office for Northern Ireland
(02890 252000)
General Register Office for Scotland
(0131 3340380)

VENUE-FINDING SERVICES

Noble's Wedding Venues Guide
Information on over 2,000 civil wedding and reception venues in England and Wales. Call 01580 752404 to order a copy.

Alternative Occasions
(01932 872115)
Countrywide.
Country House Wedding Venues
(01244 571208)
Countrywide.
Virgin Bride
(020 7766 9109)
London area.

MARQUEE HIRE

Many of the companies listed offer a nationwide service; call to check.

Andrassy Marquees
(01709 889800)
Belle Tents
(01840 261556)
Berry Marquees
(01372 379814)
CBC Marquees
(01179 801120)
Field & Lawn Marquees
(01506 857938)
Inside Outside Marquee Hire
(01372 459485)
James Fletchers Marquee Hire
(01388 527658)
London Garden Marquees
(020 8672 2580)
Past Tents
(01623 862480)
Historical designs.
Purvis Marquee Hire
(0131 5541331)
Raj Tent Club
(020 7376 9066)
Rajasthani designs.

MARQUEE LININGS & DECORATIONS

Crescent Moon
(01373 830094)
Starlight Design
(020 8960 6078)
Starry-sky linings.

FLORISTS

Candida French
131e Kensington
  Church Street
London W8 7LP
(020 7792 4858)
The Country Garden
Llanrhydd Mill
Ruthin
Clywd
(01824 705179)
Edward Goodyear
at Claridge's
Brook Street
London W1A 2JQ
(020 7629 1508)
The Flower Van
81 Fulham Road
London SW3 6RD
(020 7589 1852)
Hilary Florist
74 Cardiff Road
Caerphilly CF83 1JR
(02920 886300)
Jane Packer
56 James Street
London W1U 1HF
(020 7935 2673)
Kenneth Turner
8 Avery Row
London W1K 4AL
(020 7355 3880)

Lavender Green
12 Bridgewater Way
Windsor
Berkshire SL4 1RD
(01753 831112)
Margaret Bleasdale
Harrogate
(01423 502720)
Margaret Mason
85 Friargate
Preston
Lancashire PR1 2ED
(01772 253858)
Mary Jane Vaughan
Design at Fast Flowers
609 Fulham Road
London SW6 5UA
(020 7385 8400)
Michael Pooley Flowers
21 Arlington Way
London EC1R 1UY
(020 7833 5599)
Nicky Llewellyn Flowers
Somerset
(01458 223524)
Parterre
8 Marylebone Passage
London W1W 8EX
(020 7323 1623)
Paula Pryke Flowers
20 Penton Street
London N1 9PS
(020 7837 7336)
Pulbrook & Gould
Liscartan House
127 Sloane Street
London SW1X 9AS
(020 7730 0030)
Roots, Fruits & Flowers
451 Great Western Road
Glasgow G12 8HH
(0141 3395817)

Shane Connolly
London
(020 8964 4398)
Simon Lycett
London
(020 8874 1040)
Tiger Rose Floral Design
Hampshire
(01730 829989)
Veevers Carter Flowers
(020 7735 1400)
Nationwide.

FLOWER PRESERVATION

Perpetuelles
(01829 751225)
Chester and surrounds.
Petals & Lace
(01371 873986)
Mail order.
Pressed Flower Designs
(01273 424299)
South-East England.
Pressed for Time
(01489 574668)
Mail order.
Rhapsody in Bloom
(01792 893214)
Mail order.
Steffano Flowers
(07961 132891)
Nationwide.

MUSIC

**The Incorporated
Society of Musicians**
(020 7629 4413)
Can recommend
classical ensembles.
Produces a leaflet,
Music for a Wedding.

CDS OF WEDDING MUSIC

*Music For a Civil Wedding
Vols I* and *II*

*Love Divine – The
Complete Guide to
Church Wedding Music*
WMC Records
(020 8314 1273)
*Music For Your Wedding –
A Complete Guide*
Priory
(01525 377566)
Mail order.
Wedding Music
New World Music
(01986 781682)
Mail order.

Many of the
companies below offer
a nationwide service;
call to check.

MUSIC AGENCIES

**Central England
Music Agency**
(0121 2488280) or
(0870 7023456)
Function Junction
(020 8900 5959)
London Music Agency
(01992 578617)
Music at Your Service
(01905 358474)
**The Professional
Musicians Network**
(020 7639 3331)
Rent-A-Band
(01924 441441)

Sternberg-Clarke
(020 8877 1102)
Also general
entertainment.
Upbeat Management
(020 8773 1223)
**The Wedding Music
Company**
(020 8293 3392)

CASINOS

Carnival Creative
Hospitality
(01895 833822)
Also general
entertainment.
Monte Carlo Casino
Entertainment
(020 8242 9793)
Monte Carlo Fun Casino
(020 7384 1489)

DISCOS

Sounds Good To Me
(020 7700 7749)

DOVES

Animal Actors
(020 8348 0320)
The White Dove
Company
(020 8508 1414)

FIREWORKS

Brilliant Fireworks
(0800 4583355)
Celebration Displays
(0161 7234422)
The Firework Company
(01884 840504)

Firework Factors
(01531 640441)
Pains Fireworks
(01794 884040)

GENERAL ENTERTAINMENT

Some of the
companies below offer
a nationwide service;
call to check.

Attention Seekers
(020 7502 6369)
Human statues and
walkabout performers.
Complete Talent Agency
(01702 427100)
Fire eaters, stilt walkers
and jugglers.
Crêchendo
(020 8772 8140)
Entertainment for
children.
The Dumb Waiters
(0121 3080237)
Comic waiters.
Fanfare 3000
(020 8429 3000)
Clowns, caricaturists
and bands.
The Jolly Jester
(01707 266769)
Jesters, jugglers, stilt
walkers and fire eaters.
NDS
(07000 637637)
General entertainment
agency.
Sarah Bailey
(01935 881927)
Caricaturist.

Susan Scott Lookalikes
(020 7387 9245)
What a Palaver!!
(01623 811467)
Medieval-style
entertainment.

PIPERS

**Highland Wedding
Day Pipers**
(02380 268835)
**International
Highlanders**
(0121 2415981)

PHOTOGRAPHY & VIDEOGRAPHY ASSOCIATIONS

**British Institute of
Professional
Photography**
(01920 464011)
www.epicentre.
co.uk/bipp
Website has a list
of members.
**The Guild of Wedding
Photographers UK**
(07000 484536)
www.gwp-uk.co.uk
The Guild produces a
useful leaflet. Its
website also has advice
and a list of members.
**Master Photographers
Association**
(01325 356555)
www.mpauk.com
Website has a list
of members.

**The Society of
Wedding and Portrait
Photographers**
(01745 815030)
www.swpp.co.uk
Website has a list
of members.

**Association of
Professional
Videomakers**
(01529 421717)
www.apv.org.uk
Website has a list of
members specializing
in wedding videos, tips
and links to other
websites.
**The Institute of
Videography**
(0845 7413626)
www.iov.co.uk
Website has a list of
members and guide to
choosing a wedding
videographer.

TRANSPORT

Some of the
companies below offer
a nationwide service,
others a more local
one. Call to check.

BUSES

London Central Buses
(020 8646 1747)
Original London
Sightseeing Tour
Company
(020 8877 1722)

BALLOONS

Virgin Balloon Flights
(01952 200141)

CARS

American 50s Car Hire
(01268 735914)
Bespokes
(01923 250250)
Carriages Vehicle
Agency
(01737 353926)
Novelty cars such
as Chitty Chitty
Bang Bang.
Cars of Character
(01494 792013)
Fleetwood Classic
Limousines
(020 7624 0869)
Greens Carriage Masters
(020 8692 9200)
Lord Cars
(020 7435 1114)
Luxury Limousines
(01759 373818)
Silver Lady Classics
(01707 326051)
Vintage Wedding Cars
(01753 883234)
White Cat Classics
(01689 852168)

COACHES & CARRIAGES

Capital Carriages
(01277 372082)
Cinderella's Magic Coach
(01491 413322)
Haydn Webb Carriages
(0118 9883334)

Orchard Poyle
Carriage Hire
(01784 435983)

HELICOPTERS

Alan Mann Helicopters
(01276 857471)
Burman Aviation
(01234 752220)

MOTORBIKES

Metropolis Motorcycles
(020 7793 9313)
Warrs
(020 7736 2934)
Windy Corner Triumph
(01455 842922)

RICKSHAWS

Wheel Alternatives
(01904 338338)

TAXIS

Austins Vintage Taxi Hire
(020 8767 0817)
White Wedding Taxis
(01959 575224)

CAKES

The British
Sugarcraft Guild
(020 8859 6943)
Can put you in touch
with cakemakers in
your area.

The companies below
may deliver locally or
nationally; call to check.

Cakes by Rachel Mount
London
(020 8672 9333)
Choccywoccydoodah
Brighton
(01273 329462)
London
(020 7724 5465)
Dunn's of Crouch End
6 The Broadway
Crouch End
London N8 9NS
(020 8340 1614)
Helen Houlden Exclusive
Cake Design
Nottingham
(0115 9333751)
Jane Asher Party Cakes
22–24 Cale Street
London SW3 3QU
(020 7584 6177)
La Patisserie Française
Pierre Pechon
127 Queensway
London W2 4SJ
(020 7221 4819)
Linda Calvert Cakes
Lewes
(01273 474739)
Maison Blanc
Chichester
(01243 539292)
Cobham
(01932 868194)
Guildford
(01483 301171)
London
(020 8838 0848)
Oxford
(01865 510974)
Marks & Spencer
(020 7935 4422)
Branches nationwide.

Pat-A-Cake Pat-A-Cake
London
(020 7485 0006)
Purita Hyam Wedding
Cakes
Sussex
(01403 891518)
Roney's Cakes of Quality
London and the
Home Counties.
(01428 652924)
Slattery
190 Bury New Road
Whitefield
Manchester M45 6QF
(0161 7679303)
Sugarflower
London
(020 8366 5907)
Sugar Surgeons
129 Beacon Street
Lichfield
Staffordshire WS13 7BG
(01543 418861)
Suzelle Cakes
10 Replingham Road
London SW18 5LS
(020 8874 4616)
Tesco
(0800 505555)
Branches nationwide.
Waitrose
(0800 188884)
Branches nationwide.

CAKEMAKING SUPPLIES

Icing World
1196 Warwick Road
Acocks Green
Birmingham B27 6BY
(0121 7062922)

Jane Asher Party Cakes
(020 7584 6177)
Mail order.
C Cake Supply
(01530 414554)
Mail order.
Squire's Kitchen
Sugarcraft
Squires House
8 Waverley Lane
Farnham
Surrey GU9 8SB
(01252 734309)
Also mail order.

CATERERS & PARTY PLANNERS

Many of the
companies below offer
a nationwide service;
call to check.

M & PM Catering
(020 8789 4447)
The Admirable Crichton
(020 7733 8113)
Annie Fryer Catering
(020 7352 7693)
By Word of Mouth
(020 8871 9566)
The Wintons
(020 8871 4110)
Fifth Element
Event Design
(020 7610 8630)
Orange on The Move
(020 7263 5000)
Mosimann's Party
Service
(020 7326 8344)
Mustard Catering
(020 7840 5900)

Norman & Hatwell
(01963 362856)
Party Planners
(020 7229 9666)
Rhubarb Food Design
(020 7738 9272)
Simply Delicious
(01653 692725)
Table Talk
(020 7401 3200)
21st Century Food
(020 8960 3119)
**William Bartholomew
Party Organising**
(020 7731 8328)

CATERING HIRE

All the companies
below offer a
nationwide service.

Jones Hire
(020 7735 5577)
Jongor Events
(0800 3899999)
Just Hire
(020 8595 8855)
Mitchell Linen Hire
(020 8346 0330)
Planner Catering
(020 7987 2102)

TOASTMASTERS

The Guild of Professional
Toastmasters
(020 8852 4621)
**The National Association
of Toastmasters**
(01634 402684)

BALLOONS

The Balloon & Kite
Company
613 Garratt Lane
London SW18 4SU
(020 8946 5962)
Also mail order.
Balloon Boom
London
(020 7254 1068)
The Balloon Shop
332 Baker Street
Enfield
Middlesex EN1 3LH
(020 8363 2670)
B-Loony
(01494 774376)
Mail order.
Folkdean
(01594 841545)
Mail order.

CANDLES

Price's Patent Candle
Company
(020 7228 3345)
Stocked nationwide.
Wax Lyrical
(020 8561 0235)
Branches nationwide.

All the companies
below offer a mail-
order service.

CONFETTI

Glittering Wishes
(01273 424299)
The Very Nice Company
(01884 841136)

BUBBLES

Celebrations
(01332 342600)
Forever Memories
(01384 878111)
Wedding Bubbles
(01288 353838)

FLOWER-PETAL CONFETTI

Celebrations
(01332 342600)
**The Real Flower Petal
Confetti Company**
(01386 555045)
Rhapsody in Bloom
(01792 893214)
The Very Nice Company
(01884 841136)

FAVOURS

Almond Art
(0800 2985673)
**Bomboniere by
Manancourt**
(01780 751926)
Bomboniere by Natalie
(020 8202 6579)
Carte Blanche Creations
(01943 600283)
Celebrations
(01332 342600)
Forever Memories
(01384 878111)
RTL
(01592 263352)
Personalized whisky,
brandy and vodka
miniatures.
Sophie's Chocolates
(01494 782999)

The Very Nice Company
(01884 841136)
With Love From
(01727 812226)

CRACKERS

Absolutely Crackers
(01908 236227)
Totally Crackers
(0113 2785525)

DISPOSABLE CAMERAS

Forever Memories
(01384 878111)
Picture Perfect Cameras
(0800 0747409)
The Wedding
Camera Store
(020 8673 5852)

GIFT-LIST COMPANIES

Many of the
companies below have
catalogues or internet
sites, so you don't have
to visit them in person.
Call to check.

Trading Direct
Unit E4
The Old Imperial
   Laundry
71 Warriner Gardens
London SW11 4XW
(01672 516633)
www.trading-
   direct.co.uk
By appointment.

The Wedding List
91 Walton Street
London SW3 2HP
(020 7584 1222)
www.theweddinglist.
   org.uk
Wedding List Services
127 Queenstown Road,
London SW8 3RH
(020 7978 1118)
www.wedding.co.uk
The Wedding Shop
171 Fulham Road
London SW3 6JW
(020 7751 0888)

37 Blandford Street
London W1V 7HB
(020 7935 3100)
www.wedshop.co.uk
www.confetti.co.uk
(0870 8406060)
Mail order or online
shopping only.

GIFT LISTS: GENERAL STORES

Allders
(0870 0010337)
www.allders.com
Branches nationwide.
Argos
(01908 600557)
www.argos.co.uk
Branches nationwide.
Debenhams
(020 7408 4444)
www.debenhams.com
Branches nationwide.
Habitat
(020 7255 6045)
www.habitat.net
Branches nationwide.

Heal's
(020 7636 1666)
www.heals.co.uk
London and Surrey.
House of Fraser
(020 7734 7070)
www.houseof
   fraser.co.uk
Branches nationwide.
John Lewis
Oxford Street
London W1A 1EX
(020 7629 7711)
www.johnlewis.co.uk
Also branches
nationwide.
Liberty
210–220 Regent Street
London W1R 6AH
(020 7573 9533)
www.liberty.co.uk
Marks & Spencer
(01925 858502)
www.marksand
   spencer.com
Branches nationwide.
Selfridges
400 Oxford Street
London W1A 1AB
(020 7318 3260)

1 The Dome
The Trafford Centre
Manchester M17 8DA
(0161 6291234)
www.selfridges.co.uk

GIFT LISTS: SPECIALIST COMPANIES

Bridgewater
81a Marylebone High
   Street
London W1U 4QL
(020 7486 6897)

28a Dundas Street
Edinburgh EH3 6JN
(0131 5569781)
Pottery.
British Airways
(0845 6060747)
Travel vouchers to use
for honeymoons and
weddings abroad, from
its travel shops.
Christofle
10 Hanover Street
London W1S 1YG
(020 7491 4004)
Crystal and china.
Designers Guild
267 King's Road
London SW3 5EN
(020 7351 5775)
Homeware.
Divertimenti
139–141 Fulham Road
London SW3 6SD
(020 7581 8065)

45–47 Wigmore Street
London W1V 1PS
(020 7935 0689)
Kitchenware.
Edinburgh Crystal
(01968 672244)
Nationwide.
Crystal.

Mulberry Hall
>tonegate
York YO1 8ZW
01904 620736)
Also mail order.
China, glass and
utlery.
Ocean
0870 8484840).
Catalogue/mail order.
Homeware.
oyal Doulton
01782 292165)
Nationwide.
China.
oyal Worcester Spode
01782 744011)
Nationwide.
china.
mall Island Trader
www.smallisland
trader.com
china and glass.
homas Cook
870 7502222)
ouchers which can be
sed for honeymoons
r weddings abroad.
homas Goode
9 South Audley Street
ondon W1Y 6BN
20 7493 4996)
hina, glass and
omeware.
edgwood
8000 280026)
ationwide.
hina.
e White House
2 Waterford Road
ondon SW6 2HA
20 7629 3521)
ecorative and
ousehold linen.

HONEYMOONS AND WEDDINGS ABROAD: TOUR OPERATORS

Abercrombie & Kent
(0845 0700600)
Airtours
(0870 2412567)
Austravel
(020 7734 7755)
Bales Worldwide
(01306 732718)
British Airways Holidays
(0870 2424245)
British Airways Holidays
Weddings
(01293 722648)
Cadogan Holidays
(02380 828313)
Caribbean Connection
(0870 751930)
Caribbean Expressions
(020 7431 2131)
Caribtours
(020 7751 0660)
Cazenove & Loyd Safaris
(020 8875 9666)
Citalia
(020 8686 5533)
Cosmos
(0161 4765678)
Cosmos Dream
Weddings
(0870 2646020)
Couples
(020 8900 1913)
Cox & Kings
(020 7873 5000)
Elegant Resorts
(01244 350408)
First Choice
(0870 7500100)

First Choice Wedding
Collection
(0161 7422262)
Greaves Travel
(020 7487 5687)
Harlequin Travel
(01708 850300)
Hayes & Jarvis
(0870 8989890)
Kuoni Weddings
(01306 747007)
Lunn Poly
(0870 3334400)
Magic Travel Group
(020 8939 5439)
Magical Mauritius
(01488 668821)
Sandals Resorts
(0800 742742)
Scott Dunn World
(020 8672 1234)
Seasons in Style
(0870 0732766)
Sovereign Holidays
(0870 6070770)
Sun International
(01491 411222)
Hotelier.
SuperClubs
(020 8339 4150)
Hotelier.
Swept Away Resorts
(020 8900 1913)
Thomas Cook Faraway
(01733 418450)
Thomson
(0870 6080169)
Tradewinds Worldwide
Holidays
(0870 7510009)
Trailfinders
(020 7938 3939)
(020 7937 5400)

Tropical Places
(0800 0185256)
Tropical Places
Weddings
(01342 825123)
Union-Castle Travel
(020 7229 1411)
Virgin Holidays
(01293 617181)
Virgin Holidays
Weddings
(01293 744265)
Weddings &
Honeymoons Abroad
(0161 9691122)
Western & Oriental
(020 7313 6600)
Worldwide Journeys &
Expeditions
(020 7386 4646)

HONEYMOON FASHION

All the labels below are
stocked nationwide.

Brides of Paradise
(0121 7081841)
Oceanna by
Helen Marina
(020 8361 3777)
Victoria Jane by
Ronald Joyce
(020 7636 8989)

CAKES

Pat-A-Cake Pat-A-Cake
(020 7485 0006)
Produces a range of
small wedding cakes
packaged to be carried
as hand luggage.

The publisher would like to thank the following for items used in photographing this book.

Alastair Lockhart
91 Walton Street
London SW3 2HP
(020 7581 8289)

Beverley Hills
108 Hatton Garden
London EC1N 8LY
(020 7405 4847)

Butler & Wilson
20 South Molton Street
London W1K 5QU
(020 7409 2955)

Butterfly
70 New Kings Road
London SW6 4LT
(020 7371 9291)

Damask
3–4 Broxholme House
New Kings Road
London SW6 4AA
(020 7731 3553)

Dinny Hall
54 Fulham Road
London SW3 6HH
(020 7589 9192)

Fast Flowers
609 Fulham Road
London SW6 5UA
(020 7381 6422)

Heal's
196 Tottenham Court
Road
London W1P 9LD
(020 7636 1666)

Homes in Heaven
72 New Kings Road
London SW6 4LT
(020 7736 2227)

Jerry's Home Store
163–167 Fulham Road
London SW3 6SN
(020 7581 0909)

Jess James
3 Newburgh Street
London W1F 7RB
(020 7437 0199)

Kara Kara
2a Pond Place
London SW3 6QJ
(020 7591 0891)

Kiki McDonough
77c Walton Street
London SW3 2HT
(020 7581 1777)

Nina Campbell
9 Walton Street
London SW3 2JD
(020 7225 0644)

Paperchase
213–215 Tottenham
Court Road
London W1T 7PS
(020 7467 6200)

Papyrus
48 Fulham Road
London SW3 6HH
(020 7584 8022)

Sifani
166 Walton Street
London SW3 2JL
(020 7838 0160)

Smythson of Bond Street
40 New Bond Street
London W1S 2DE
(020 7629 8558)

Susan O'Hanlon
(01753 887529)
Wedding stationery.

Thomas Goode
19 South Audley Street
London W1Y 6BN
(020 7629 4230)

The Wedding List
91 Walton Street
London SW3 2HP
(020 7584 1222)

Every effort has been made to ensure the information on these pages is correct. Please let the publishers know of any changes. W would be pleased to make alterations in future editions of this book.

PICTURE
CREDITS

Key: ph – photographer,
a – above, b – below,
c – centre, l – left, r – right

Endpapers ph Caroline Arber;
1 ph Caroline Arber; 2–3 ph
Caroline Arber; 4–5 ph
Caroline Arber; 7 ph Polly
Wreford, except tl ph
Caroline Arber; 8 t, cr, br & cl
ph Caroline Arber; 10–11 ph
Caroline Arber; 12–13 ph
Polly Wreford; 14–19 ph Polly
Wreford; 20–25 ph Caroline
Arber; 27 ph Caroline Arber,
except br ph Polly Wreford;
28–36 ph Caroline Arber;
37 ph Caroline Arber, except
br ph Polly Wreford; 38 ph
Caroline Arber; 40–41 ph
Polly Wreford; 42–51 ph
Caroline Arber; 52 ph
Caroline Arber; 53–54 ph
Caroline Arber; 55–57 ph
Viv Yeo; 58–60 ph Caroline
Arber; 61 ph Viv Yeo; 62–62
ph Caroline Arber; 64 l ph
Viv Yeo; 64 r ph Caroline
Arber; 65 ph Caroline Arber;
66 tl ph Viv Yeo; 66 cl ph
Polly Wreford; 66 bl ph

Caroline Arber; 67 ph Polly
Wreford; 68–69 ph Caroline
Arber; 70 l ph Viv Yeo; 70 r
ph Caroline Arber; 71 l ph
Caroline Arber; 71 r ph
Caroline Arber; 72–73 ph
Polly Wreford; 74–76 ph
Caroline Arber; 77 ph
Caroline Arber; 78 ph Polly
Wreford; 79–80 ph Caroline
Arber; 82–83 ph Polly
Wreford; 84 ph Caroline
Arber; 85 tr ph Viv Yeo; 85 br
Polly Wreford; 86–87 ph
Caroline Arber; 88 ph Polly
Wreford; 89 ph Caroline
Arber; 90 ph Caroline Arber;
91–92 ph Polly Wreford;
95 t ph Caroline Arber;
95 b ph Viv Yeo; 96–97 ph
Caroline Arber; 99 ph Polly
Wreford; 100–103 ph Caroline
Arber; 105 ph Polly Wreford;
106–107 ph Caroline Arber;
108–111 ph Polly Wreford;
112 ph Caroline Arber;
113–119 ph Polly Wreford;
120–129 ph Caroline Arber;
130 ph Simon Upton / A
house in Morocco designed
by Elie Mouyal; 131 ph Jan
Baldwin; 132 ph Simon
Upton / A house in Morocco

designed by Elie Mouyal;
133 r ph Simon Upton /
Interior design by Todhunter
Earle Interiors; 133 l ph Jan
Baldwin; 134 l ph Simon
Upton / A house in Morocco
designed by François Gilles;
134 r ph Simon Upton;
135–137 ph Simon Upton;
160 ph Caroline Arber.

BUSINESS CREDITS

François Gilles
IPL Interiors
t. 020 7622 3009

Todhunter Earle Interiors
t. 020 7349 9999

Elie Mouyal
Architect
t. + 212 430 0502

WEDDING CREDITS

The publisher would like to thank everyone who made the photography for this book possible. Special thanks to David and Annabel, Lizzie and Justin, and Jamie and Berenice for graciously allowing us to photograph their beautiful weddings.

THE WEDDING OF DAVID AND ANNABEL

Wedding Venue
The Vineyard at Stockcross
Newbury
Berkshire RG20 8JU
t. 01635 528770
page: 95

Thanks to Billy Read – Executive Chef and Eduardo Armadi – Sommelier, at The Vineyard. Thanks to Zak Jones (Best Man), Jo Simmonds & Vicky Sutton (Attendants), Amy Weeks (Flower Girl), John and Rosemary Sutton and Brian and Diane Taylor (Parents).

THE WEDDING OF LIZZIE AND JUSTIN

Wedding Dress Designer
Sophie English
68a Rochester Row
London SW1P 1JU
t. 020 7828 9007
f. 020 7630 8396
e. enquiries@sophie-
  english.co.uk
page: 65

Bridesmaid Dress
Kiss The Frog!
Mill Lane Studio
Mill Lane
Godalming
Surrey GU7 1EY
t. 01483 416406
f. 01483 419504
pages: 58–59

Flowers
Hazel Anne
2 Quarry Cottages
Wall Hill Road
Ashurstwood
Sussex RH19 3TQ
t. 01342 823728
pages: 84, 86 t

THE WEDDING OF JAMIE AND BERENICE

Wedding Dress Designer
Jane Law
57 First Avenue
Worthing
Sussex BN14 9NP
t. 01903 207472
pages: 62–63

Flowers
Jane Durbridge
Parterre
8 Marylebone Passage
London W1W 8EX
t. 020 7323 1623
pages: 2, 74–75, 90, 106–1

Cake Designer
Corinna Rittner
29 Kelso Place
London W8 5AG
t. 020 7938 3164
page: 112